Eyewitness
PYRAMID

Written by
JAMES PUTNAM

Photographed by
GEOFF BRIGHTLING AND PETER HAYMAN

Hetepheres and
her husband
Katep, C. 2500 B.C

Two plaques
with name of
Nubian king
Aspelta

Dorling Kindersley

Carving from tomb of Ti, Saqqara

Falcon
jewellery

LONDON, NEW YORK, MUNICH,
MELBOURNE, and DELHI

Project editor Scott Steedman
Art editor Manisha Patel
Managing editor Simon Adams
Managing art editor Julia Harris
Production Catherine Semark
Researcher Céline Carez
Picture research Cynthia Hole
Editorial consultant Dr I.E.S. Edwards

PAPERBACK EDITION
Managing editor Andrew Macintyre
Managing art editor Jane Thomas
Editor and reference compiler Lorrie Mack
Art editor Rebecca Johns
Production Jenny Jacoby
Picture research Angela Anderson
DTP designer Siu Ho

This Eyewitness ® Guide has been conceived by
Dorling Kindersley Limited and Editions Gallimard

Hardback edition first published in Great Britain in 1994.
This edition published in Great Britain in 2002
by Dorling Kindersley Limited,
80 Strand, London WC2R ORL

Copyright © 1994, © 2002, Dorling Kindersley Limited, London
A Pearson Company

A CIP catalogue record for this book is
available from the British Library.

ISBN-13: 978 0 7513 4744 9

Colour reproduction by
Colourscan, Singapore
Printed in Hong Kong by Toppan

See our complete
catalogue at

www.dk.com

Nubian pot decorated
with blue lotuses

Jewellery found near the
pyramid of Senusret III,
1874–1855 B.C

Shabti figure of King Aspelta
of Nubia, 593–568 B.C.

Model of King
Khufu's funerary boat

Contents

Tomb model of workers making mud bricks

What are pyramids?

THE PYRAMIDS OF EGYPT have fascinated people for thousands of years. How did the ancient Egyptians build these massive stone monuments, and why? The most famous pyramids are the three at Giza, near modern Cairo. But there are more than 80 other pyramids in Egypt, and another 100 further south in the Sudan. Each one is a tomb, built by a pharaoh (king) as the final resting place for his body. The pyramid was meant to help the dead pharaoh achieve eternal life. But we may never know why the Egyptians chose the pyramid shape. It may have developed from early burial mounds, or been a symbol of the sun's rays or a stairway to heaven. Many centuries later, the people of Central America also built pyramids, mainly as temples. Hundreds of these are still hidden in the deep jungles.

THE GREAT SPHINX
The period we call ancient Egypt lasted for 3,000 years. The Giza pyramids and the Sphinx (pp. 26–27) were built early on, during the Old Kingdom (c. 2686–2181 B.C.). Pyramid building was revived in the Middle Kingdom (2055–1650 B.C.). By the New Kingdom (1550–1069 B.C.), pharaohs (including Tutankhamun) were buried in more secret rock tombs.

MOUNTAIN PEAKS
Holy buildings all over the world have a pointed pyramid shape. Mo cultures believe the gods live in the heavens, so earthly spirits can rise from temples to join them. Most temples, churches, synagogues, mosques, and pagodas have spires that rise like mountain peaks. This the Temple of Siva in Prambana in Java, Indonesia.

BLOODTHIRSTY SACRIFICE
The Aztecs of ancient Mexico built pyramid temples to worship their gods (pp. 60–61). These had two staircases that led to two shrines. Here Aztec priests performed human sacrifices in honour of the forces of nature. They believed they could only keep the sun alive if they fed the gods with human blood.

Aztec, Mayan, and other Central American pyramids

Egyptian and Sudanese pyramids

WORLDS APART
Pyramids are found in Egypt and Central America. But there is no evidence that the early Americans had any contact with Egypt, or even knew that the Egyptian pyramids existed. In both time and space, the two civilizations were worlds apart.

SPOT THE DIFFERENCE
This is the Mayan pyramid of Chichén Itzá in Mexico. Central American pyramids have flat tops and staircases on at least one side. Mayan priests climbed the stairs to reach the altar on the summit. Unlike the best Egyptian pyramids, which are made of solid limestone blocks, Central American pyramids are filled with layers of rubble.

STONE SUNBEAM
The pharaoh Khafra built this pyramid at Giza around 2530 B.C. It is only slightly smaller than the Great Pyramid, the biggest of them all (pp. 22–23). The pyramid shape resembles the rays of the sun shining through a break in the clouds. The tip may have been cased in gold to make it shine like the sun.

HIDDEN MOUND
The earliest Egyptian tombs were burial mounds. A simple grave was covered with a heap of gravel, to protect it and mark the spot in the shifting desert sands. Later on, kings and high officials were buried in mastabas, oblong buildings made of sun-dried mud bricks. Some mastabas had sand mounds overlaid with bricks over the burial chamber. This is the Step Pyramid of King Djoser, built around 2650 B.C. (pp. 12–15). It was the first pyramid, and the first king's tomb made of stone.

CHANGING SHAPE
The first Egyptian pyramids had stepped sides. These probably represented a stairway which the dead king could climb to join the other gods among the stars (pp. 22, 47). Later the sun became more important than the stars in Egyptian religion. Then they built true pyramids with sloping sides representing the sun's rays. This is the ruined Meidum Pyramid (pp. 14–15), which was between the two. It started life as a step pyramid, and was later modified to become a true pyramid.

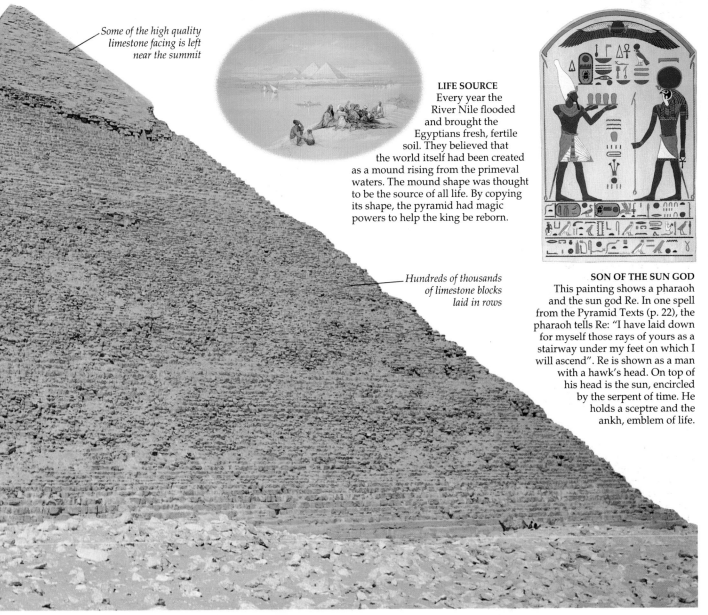

Some of the high quality limestone facing is left near the summit

Hundreds of thousands of limestone blocks laid in rows

LIFE SOURCE
Every year the River Nile flooded and brought the Egyptians fresh, fertile soil. They believed that the world itself had been created as a mound rising from the primeval waters. The mound shape was thought to be the source of all life. By copying its shape, the pyramid had magic powers to help the king be reborn.

SON OF THE SUN GOD
This painting shows a pharaoh and the sun god Re. In one spell from the Pyramid Texts (p. 22), the pharaoh tells Re: "I have laid down for myself those rays of yours as a stairway under my feet on which I will ascend". Re is shown as a man with a hawk's head. On top of his head is the sun, encircled by the serpent of time. He holds a sceptre and the ankh, emblem of life.

Built for a king

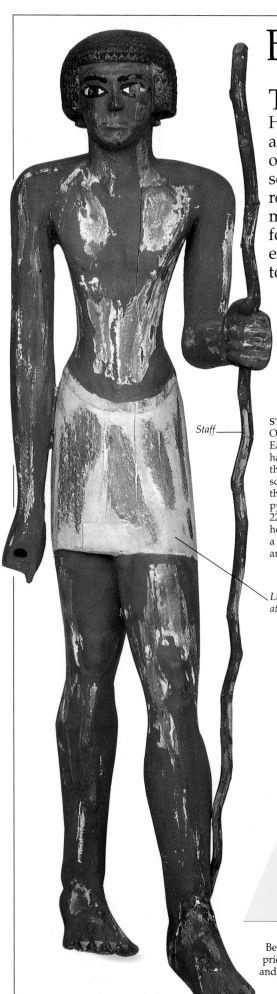

THE EGYPTIANS BELIEVED THEIR PHARAOH was a living god. He led the army in battle, passed judgement on criminals, and controlled the treasury. He also represented the unity of Egypt. In early times, most people lived in the north or the south, called Lower and Upper Egypt. It was the pharaoh's role to keep the two regions together. The centralized government meant he had all the resources of Egypt at his disposal for building his pyramid. The finest sculptors, masons, engineers, and countless workers spent years building the tomb. The labourers who dragged the stones were not slaves. They were farmers who believed that if they helped their king get to heaven, he would look after them in the next world.

STAFF OF OFFICE
Officials were very powerful. Each government department had a large staff, ranging from the chief official to many scribes. Officials often built their tombs around the king's pyramid. This statue from 2250 B.C. shows an official holding a wooden staff, a sign of his rank and authority.

Staff

Linen kilt tied at the waist

PYRAMID SITES
There are more than 80 pyramids in Egypt. They are all on the west bank of the Nile, where the sun sets. In the Old Kingdom, pyramids were grouped around Memphis, the capital. In the Middle Kingdom, the capital was moved upriver to Lisht, so most pharaohs built their pyramids further south.

Cairo

Abu Roash ▲
Giza ▲▲▲
Zawyet el-Aryan ▲▲▲
Abusir ▲▲ ▲
Saqqara ▲▲▲▲ ▲▲▲▲
Dahshur ▲▲ ▲▲▲▲
Mazghuna ▲ ▲

KEY
▲ True pyramid
▲ Bent pyramid
▰ Step pyramid

Lisht ▲ ▲

Seila ▰   ▲ Meidum

River Nile

▲ Hawara
▲ El Lahun

Pharaoh

Nobles and royalty, important officials, soldiers, scribes

Skilled craftsworkers, painters, sculptors, overseers, merchants

Agricultural workers, domestic servants (there were very few slaves)

THE SOCIAL PYRAMID
Beneath the pharaoh were the royal family, nobles, and important priests, soldiers, and officials. The middle class included merchants and skilled craftsworkers. But most Egyptians were peasant farmers.

SON OF THE SUN GOD
The pharaoh had many official titles, including Lord of the Two Lands and Son of Re, the sun god. This huge head of Radjedef was found near his pyramid at Abu Roash. The king is wearing the royal *nemes* headcloth. A cobra is poised on his brow, ready to spit fire at the king's enemies. Radjedef only ruled for eight years, between Khufu and Khafra, who built the two massive pyramids at Giza. His pyramid is ruined.

Ancient Egyptian women carried trays and baskets on their heads

HUMBLE SERVANT
Many young women worked as servants. We know what they looked like because model figures of servants were put into tombs so that they could work for their bosses in the next life.

ODEL COUPLE
Egyptian statues, pharaohs ually have elegant, perfect tures. Ordinary people more natural and listic. This is the court icial Katep and his fe Hetepheres. He s a good suntan, but wife has pale skin, ggesting that she ent most of her e indoors. e statue was nd in Katep's mb near e Giza ramids.

Hetepheres with her arm around her husband

Katep, who lived around 2500 B.C.

Wig

r skin is nted a e yellow

His skin is painted red

The great Step Pyramid

THE FIRST PYRAMID – probably the first large stone structure in human history – was built for the pharaoh Djoser at Saqqara around 2650 B.C. It was designed by the architect Imhotep, who became more famous than the pharaoh he worked for. The Step Pyramid is really a series of six rectangular structures set one on top of the other. Beneath it, cut deep into the underground rock, lie the burial chambers of Djoser and five members of his family. The king's vault was built of pink granite and sealed with a three-tonne plug. But it was robbed long ago – only a mummified foot was found inside.

IN THE SHADOW OF THE STEP PYRAMID
Over the following centuries, many important officials built their mastaba tombs around the mighty Step Pyramid. The walls are mostly decorated with scenes of everyday life. This carving comes from the tomb of the official Mereruka, c. 2300 B.C. It shows men carrying offerings of food, including ducks.

A BUILDER'S SKETCH
This is an ancient architectural drawing, probably made by builders working on the Step Pyramid. The vertical lines allowed them to figure out the exact angle of the building's sloping sides.

BUILT IN STAGES
The Step Pyramid was built around a core of desert stones. Imhotep changed his mind five times as the building progressed. He enlarged the original mastaba form twice before building a four-tiered pyramid structure on top. Then two more tiers were added by expanding the entire structure. It was finally faced with polished limestone to give a smooth finish.

The body of the pyramid is made of small stone blocks laid like bricks

Imhotep

More than 2,000 years after his death, the ancient Egyptians worshipped Imhotep as a god of wisdom. One writer called him "the inventor of the art of building with hewn stone". He is said to have written many books and became a sort of patron saint of scribes. He is often shown seated with a papyrus unrolled across his knees. He was also thought to be the son of the god Ptah, whose magic gave him the power to heal the sick.

Bronze statue of Imhotep, New Kingdom

UNFINISHED STATUE
This is one of three unfinished life-sized statues of Djoser found in his pyramid complex. Even in this fragmentary state, the king wears a stern expression. The spirit of a dead king was thought to emerge from the burial chamber and inhabit statues like these.

DISCOVERING THE WHEEL
How were the pyramids built? Did the Egyptians have building machines? There are many theories, but little hard evidence. This painting shows soldiers climbing a ladder on wheels. It is the only known image of a wheel from the Old Kingdom. At that time the Egyptians did not have pulleys for lifting stones.

Nemes *headcloth*

Thick wig

False beard

Fine Tura limestone facing was stolen for later buildings

THE KING'S PORTRAIT
The first life-sized portrait in history is this seated statue of King Djoser. It was found in a closed chamber attached to the north side of his pyramid. Two round holes in the wall allowed the pharaoh to see the offerings left by his worshippers. The king is wearing a *nemes* headcloth, a sign of royalty, oddly poised on top of a bushy wig. His eyes were once inlaid with rock crystal. The wear and tear of 4,700 years cannot hide the king's strong personality, seen in his fierce face, prominent cheekbones, thick lips, and heavy jaw.

One of Djoser's names in hieroglyphs

The Step Pyramid complex

HIS LIFE'S WORK
Born in 1902, Jean-Philippe Lauer is a French architect and Egyptologist. He spent 50 years reconstructing the Step Pyramid complex at Saqqara. When he began, in 1926, the ruined columns and shattered blocks of stone lay buried in the desert sand. The model on this page is the fruit of his life's work.

THE SAQQARA STEP PYRAMID was one building in a large complex. Between the pyramid and its massive enclosure wall is a series of courtyards and ceremonial buildings. With the pyramid, these are probably the first large stone buildings ever made. Many are shaped and decorated like earlier structures made of mud bricks, rushes, reeds, or wood. Though they are carved to look like real buildings, most of them are dummies, complete with fake doors. One courtyard was used for the special *sed* festival, held after Djoser had been king for many years. Crowds from all over Egypt came to watch the pharaoh run a course in the *sed* court. This makes the Step Pyramid the world's first sports arena! By finishing the course, Djoser proved that he was still fit to rule. Then he was re-crowned as king of Upper and Lower Egypt on two thrones next to the *sed* court.

KIND OF BLUE
A small underground chamber lies to the sou[...]
The king was certainly buried under the pyram[...]
so this second tomb is a[...]
mystery. The carvings a[...]
blue tiles may be a copy[...]
the decoration in Djose[...]
palace at Memphis.

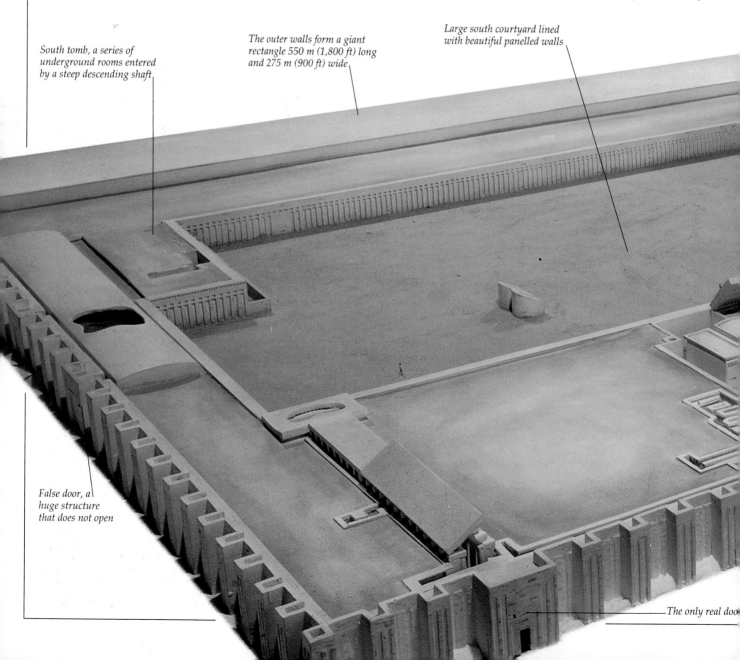

South tomb, a series of underground rooms entered by a steep descending shaft

The outer walls form a giant rectangle 550 m (1,800 ft) long and 275 m (900 ft) wide

Large south courtyard lined with beautiful panelled walls

False door, a huge structure that does not open

The only real doo[...]

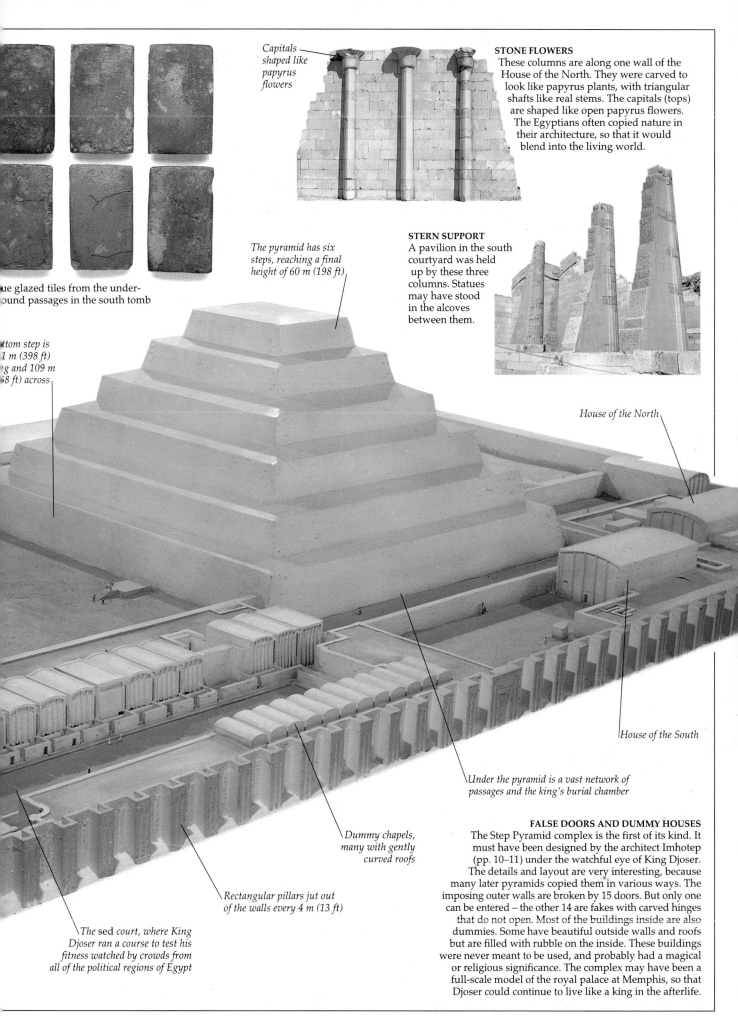

blue glazed tiles from the underground passages in the south tomb

...tom step is
...1 m (398 ft)
...g and 109 m
...8 ft) across

*The pyramid has six
steps, reaching a final
height of 60 m (198 ft)*

STONE FLOWERS

These columns are along one wall of the
House of the North. They were carved to
look like papyrus plants, with triangular
shafts like real stems. The capitals (tops)
are shaped like open papyrus flowers.
The Egyptians often copied nature in
their architecture, so that it would
blend into the living world.

*Capitals
shaped like
papyrus
flowers*

STERN SUPPORT

A pavilion in the south
courtyard was held
up by these three
columns. Statues
may have stood
in the alcoves
between them.

House of the North

House of the South

*Under the pyramid is a vast network of
passages and the king's burial chamber*

*Dummy chapels,
many with gently
curved roofs*

FALSE DOORS AND DUMMY HOUSES

The Step Pyramid complex is the first of its kind. It
must have been designed by the architect Imhotep
(pp. 10–11) under the watchful eye of King Djoser.
The details and layout are very interesting, because
many later pyramids copied them in various ways. The
imposing outer walls are broken by 15 doors. But only one
can be entered – the other 14 are fakes with carved hinges
that do not open. Most of the buildings inside are also
dummies. Some have beautiful outside walls and roofs
but are filled with rubble on the inside. These buildings
were never meant to be used, and probably had a magical
or religious significance. The complex may have been a
full-scale model of the royal palace at Memphis, so that
Djoser could continue to live like a king in the afterlife.

*Rectangular pillars jut out
of the walls every 4 m (13 ft)*

The sed *court, where King
Djoser ran a course to test his
fitness watched by crowds from
all of the political regions of Egypt*

First true pyramids

THE PHARAOHS who followed King Djoser also built step pyramids. The familiar smooth pyramid shape was not developed until the reign of King Snefer During his years as pharaoh (2613–2589 B.C.), he won wars in Libya and Nubia and built many new temples, fortresses, and palaces. Sneferu also built at least three – maybe even four – pyramids. His first, at Meidum, shows how building in stone had advanced by that time. The construction of the core and outer casing is similar to Djoser's Step Pyramid. But the builders had made great advances in handling large blocks of stone. The main structure is made of huge slabs, not many small blocks. They had also worked out a new way of roofing the burial chamber so it held the weight of the pyramid above and improved methods of sealing the entrance against robbers. All these features were used by Sneferu's son, Khufu, who built the biggest pyramid of all, the Great Pyramid of Giza. But in total tonnes of stone, Sneferu's four pyramids were an even bigger building project.

PYRAMID PROFESSOR
W. M. Flinders Petrie (1853–1942) was a brilliant English archaeologist. Over 41 years, he excavated almost every major site in Egypt. He pioneered new scientific methods and published more than a thousand books and papers. Petrie made the first detailed study of the Giza pyramids, in 1881–82. He also worked out how the strange-looking Meidum Pyramid had been built.

THE DAHSHUR PYRAMIDS
Sneferu built two large pyramids at Dahshur. It is impossible to visit them now, because they are in a military zone. This old photo shows the Bent Pyramid, which the Egyptians called "the Gleaming Pyramid of the South". It has more of its fine stone facing than any other pyramid. The builders started at a very steep pitch. But half way up they changed angles, probably because cracks appeared. The Bent Pyramid is also unusual in having two entrances and two burial chambers – both empty. The northern pyramid was built later. It is a true pyramid that rises at a very flat angle.

PRINCE...
Some of Sneferu's family were buried by the Meidum pyramid. One tomb held these superb statues of Sneferu's son Prince Rahotep and his wife Nofret.

...AND PRINCESS
The eyes are real glass. The statues are so realistic that when the workmen saw them for the first time, they dropped their tools and fled!

KILLER KING
Sneferu was the first king of the Fourth Dynasty. He was an ambitious pharaoh. This carving celebrates a raid on the turquoise mines at Maghara in the Sinai Peninsula. It shows Sneferu killing an enemy. The text calls him "a great god… who conquers the foreign lands".

FAMOUS GEESE

Sneferu's eldest son was called Nefer-Maat. He was buried with his wife Atet in a tomb next to the Meidum pyramid. The walls are painted with colourful scenes of daily life. This famous detail shows geese eating grass. Roasted geese were a great delicacy for the ancient Egyptians.

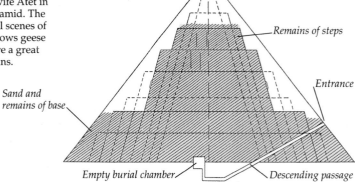

Smooth sides of true pyramid

Remains of steps

Entrance

Sand and remains of base

Empty burial chamber

Descending passage

AND ON THE INSIDE...

It is usually very hard to tell how a pyramid was made without taking it to pieces. But the Meidum Pyramid has collapsed enough to reveal its inner structure. It started off as a step pyramid with seven steps. This was later enlarged to eight. Both versions have traces of fine limestone casing and were meant to be final. But in a final change of design the steps were filled in to produce a true pyramid with smooth sides.

Meidum Pyramid stands on the border
ween green farmland, the land of the
ng, and the desert, the land of the dead

SERT TOWER

e Meidum Pyramid rises like a tower
inst the desert landscape. Only the inner
e is left, surrounded by a pile of rubble.
s picture shows the causeway leading
he entrance. This was the first pyramid
feru built, and it might have been
rted by an earlier king. Sneferu may
e decided to convert it into a true
amid when the Bent Pyramid
rted to crack. But the burial
mber was never finished.
it is further south than any
er Old Kingdom pyramid, it
y have been a cenotaph – a
morial to the dead king.

Top of the sixth step

Fifth step has been cased with fine limestone

Rough underlying stones

Rubble of sand and fallen masonry at base

The pyramids of Giza

"TIME LAUGHS AT ALL THINGS: BUT THE PYRAMIDS laugh at time". This old Arab proverb pays respect to the great pyramids of Giza, which have sat on a high plateau by the Nile for more than 4,500 years. By the time of Tutankhamun, they were more than a thousand years old, and even the Egyptians thought of them as ancient wonders. To the Arabs, who invaded Egypt in A.D. 639, the pyramids were unbelievably old. From a distance, they are an awesome, majestic sight. Up close, they are massive. The largest of the three, the Great Pyramid of King Khufu, was built around 2589 B.C. At its peak it was 147 m (481 ft) tall, with square sides 230 m (756 ft) long. It is made of about 2,300,000 blocks of solid limestone, weighing 2.5 tonnes each on average. Its neighbour, built for King Khafra, is only 3 m (9 ft) shorter. The third great pyramid was made for the pharaoh Menkaura. It is the smallest of the three, only standing 66 m (218 ft) high.

TOMBS BY THE NILE
Like all the major tombs of ancient Egypt, the Giza pyramids were built on the west bank of the River Nile. The Egyptians believed that this was the land of the dead. When the sun set in the west each day, they thought it travelled into another world where the spirits of dead kings lived.

THE RIDDLE OF THE SPHINX
The Great Sphinx (pp. 26–27) looks east towards the rising sun. Carved from a huge outcrop of limestone, it has the body of a crouching lion and the face of a king, probably Khafra. Some workers building Khafra's pyramid may have seen the shape in a piece of left-over rock. They probably carved it as a tribute to their king.

The third pyramid, built for King Menkaura around 2500 B.C.

Fine limestone and granite facing has been removed over the centuries

One of Menkaura's three "queens' pyramids"

The Giza pyramids seen from the south

BY CAMEL AROUND THE PYRAMIDS
For 4,500 years, people have come to see the great tombs of the pharaohs. Today millions of tourists from around the world visit the pyramids every year.

A GREAT VIEW
The best view of the Giza complex is from the top of the Great Pyramid. This picture comes from *Views in Egypt*, published by the Italian adventurer Luigi Mayer in 1804. It shows European travellers admiring the scenery from the summit. They are wearing Turkish dress, a common custom for travellers at the time.

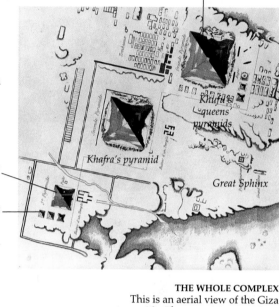

Great Pyramid of Khufu

Khufu's queens' pyramids

Khafra's pyramid

Menkaura's pyramid

Queens' pyramids

Great Sphinx

The second pyramid, built for King Khafra around 2530 B.C.

Some of the fine Tura limestone facing is left near the summit

The top 10 m (33 ft) have been lost

THE WHOLE COMPLEX
This is an aerial view of the Giza pyramids. There are 10 pyramids in all, because all three pharaohs built at least one small pyramid beside their big pyramids. These smaller structures are usually called queen's pyramids, though only some of them were built for the pharaohs' wives (p. 19).

The Great Pyramid, biggest of them all, built for King Khufu around 2589 B.C.

The pharaohs of Giza

THE PHARAOH HAD TOTAL authority. His subjects thought of him as a god and would do anything for him. Without this absolute power, the pyramids could never have been built. The word *pharaoh* means "great house", and originally referred to the palace rather than the king. Khufu, Khafra, and Menkaura had their palaces at Memphis. From there they could admire their massive tombs being built nearby at Giza. The building process took many years – if the pharaoh was lucky, his pyramid would be ready before he died. These huge projects must have put an enormous strain on Egypt's economy. When they were finally finished, the Giza pyramids were given names which celebrated the majesty of the kings who built them. The Great Pyramid was called "Khufu is one belonging to the horizon". The other two were known as "Great is Khafra" and "Menkaura is divine".

RARE PORTRAIT
Khufu was probably the most powerful pharaoh ever to rule Egypt. Yet the only portrait of him to survive is this tiny ivory statue. When it was found, it had no head. The English archaeologist Flinders Petrie had to sift through mounds of rubble before he finally found the missing head.

Pleated nem headcl

Royal be

LION THRONE
One of the most beautiful Egyptian statues is this portrait of the pharaoh Khafra. He succeeded Khufu as king, and may have been Khufu's younger brother. The statue is carved from a shiny, mottled stone called diorite. The king is shown larger than life size sitting on a lion throne. The statue was found deep in a pit in Khafra's valley temple, part of his pyramid complex. It may have been hidden there to save it from destruction by thieves or enemies.

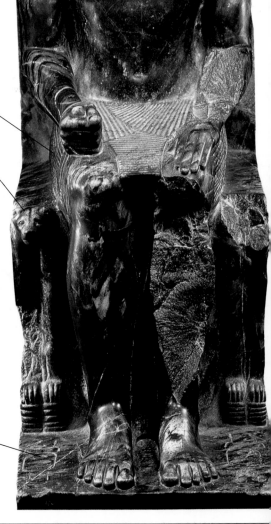

Pleated kilt

Lion head

FALCON POWER
A falcon perches on Khafra's throne, its outstretched wings wrapped around his throat. The bird represents Horus, the god associated with the supreme power and strength of the pharaoh.

HEAD IN THE SAND
The Great Sphinx (pp. 26–27) crouches in front of Khafra's pyramid. Its massive head is thought to be a portrait of the pharaoh. For most of its history, the Sphinx has been covered up to the neck in the drifting desert sands.

WE THREE KINGS
These are the cartouches – hieroglyphic names – of the three Giza pharaohs. Each name is framed by an oval loop of rope with a knot at the base. The loop represented eternity. By placing his name inside it, the pharaoh hoped to live forever.

Khafra's cartouche

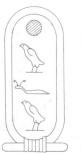

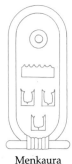

Khufu   Khafra   Menkaura

The king has a muscular physique,
while his queen has much softer curves

The fine grain of
the stone, greywacke,
gives the sculpture a
smooth finish

WHO'S YOUR FATHER?

Writing 2,000 years after the
pyramids were built, ancient
Greek historians claimed that
Menkaura was Khufu's son.
But he looks like Khafra, and
many experts now believe
Khafra was his father.
This painting shows
Menkaura as he may
have looked in life.

MODEL COUPLE

Most Egyptian pharaohs had
many wives. But only two or three
were queens, and the king usually
had a favourite. This is the earliest
known statue of a king and queen
together. They are Menkaura and his
favourite wife, Khamerernebty. The
queen is hugging her husband in an
affectionate way. Human touches like
this are rare in Egyptian art, which is
very formal. There are no records
about Menkaura from his own age.
But Greek historians say he was a
fair and just pharaoh. In contrast,
they describe Khufu and Khafra as
wicked tyrants who forced the whole
country to work on their pyramids.

Menkaura's cartouche

...CIENT REPAIRS

...roken wooden coffin was found in
...nkaura's pyramid. But the style and
...ting show that it was made nearly
...0 years after the king's death. Later
...ptians must have tried to repair
...coffin after it was damaged.

...Queens' pyramids

...ng Menkaura built three smaller pyramids
...t south of his own pyramid. None of them
...s finished, but one is partly cased in granite.
...is is the largest of the three, where his queen
...amerernebty was probably buried. Many
...er pyramid complexes include smaller
...ueens' pyramids". But not all of them were
...ilt as tombs for the king's wives. Some were
...mbs for his daughters, and others seem to
...ve had different, symbolic purposes.

The Great Pyramid

THE LARGEST AND MOST FAMOUS PYRAMID is the Great Pyramid at Giza. It was built for King Khufu around 2589 B.C. Tourists have come to marvel at it for the last 4,500 years. With its original casing of white limestone glittering in the sunlight, it must have been a truly awesome sight. Many people believe it is the greatest monument ever made. The base is bigger than any temple, cathedral, or mosque. Until the Eiffel Tower was finished in 1887, the Great Pyramid was also the tallest structure ever built. The precision of its construction is astonishing. The four sides, each slightly more than 230 m (755 ft) long, are aligned almost exactly with true north, south, east, and west. The difference between the longest and shortest sides is only 20 cm (7.9 in). This mountain of stone contains approximately 2,300,000 blocks, weighing a total of about 6,500,000 tonnes. Inside is a fascinating network of passages, shafts, galleries, and hidden chambers (pp. 22–23).

CLIMBING THE MOUNTAIN
The Arabs used to call the Great Pyram "the Mountain of Pharaoh". In the 19th century, European tourists paid local guides to carry them to the top. This wa very dangerous – people who slipped a fell were often killed. Writing in 1875, t American author Mark Twain said it wa "a lively, exhilarating, lacerating, musc straining, bone-wrenching and perfectl excruciating and exhausting pastime". Nowadays climbing the pyramids is against the law.

ANCIENT AND MODERN
Giza is now a suburb of the huge modern city of Cairo. This photo shows a Muslim cemetery built next to the Great Pyramid. Khufu's boat museum (p. 29) can be seen against the pyramid. Pollution from cars and factories is damaging the ancient stones. The foundations of the Great Pyramid are shaken every day by the constant flow of buses carrying thousands and thousands of tourists.

The pyramid's sides rise at an angle of 51.5 degrees to the peak, which was originally 147 m (481 ft) above the desert sands

HUNDREDS AND THOUSANDS
The Great Pyramid is the largest stone structure ever built. It is impossible to count all the blocks, so the total number can only be guessed at. At the core is an outcrop of rock that was incorporated in the base. The outer casing blocks were so skillfully laid that a knife blade will not slip between them.

AND ON THE INSIDE...
Khufu was probably buried in the King's Chamber, in the very heart of his pyramid. This room is lined with shiny red granite. It was robbed long ago, but still contains a sarcophagus. This is slightly larger than the door, and must have been put there as the pyramid was being built.

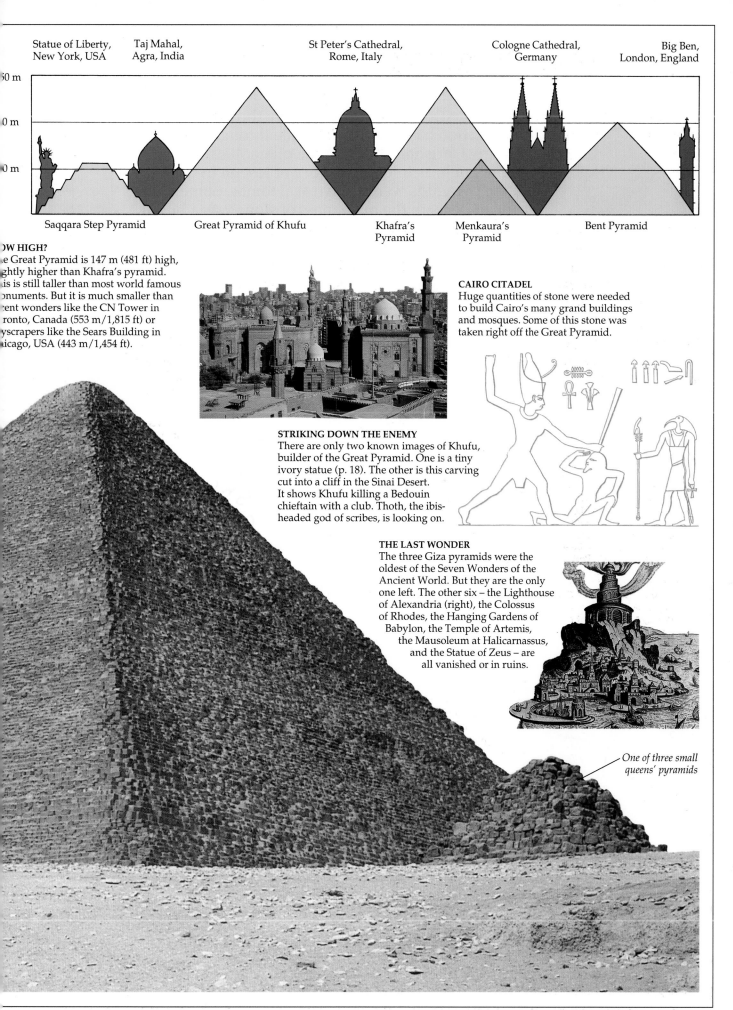

Statue of Liberty, New York, USA

Taj Mahal, Agra, India

St Peter's Cathedral, Rome, Italy

Cologne Cathedral, Germany

Big Ben, London, England

50 m

0 m

0 m

Saqqara Step Pyramid

Great Pyramid of Khufu

Khafra's Pyramid

Menkaura's Pyramid

Bent Pyramid

OW HIGH?

e Great Pyramid is 147 m (481 ft) high, ghtly higher than Khafra's pyramid. is is still taller than most world famous onuments. But it is much smaller than cent wonders like the CN Tower in ronto, Canada (553 m/1,815 ft) or yscrapers like the Sears Building in icago, USA (443 m/1,454 ft).

CAIRO CITADEL
Huge quantities of stone were needed to build Cairo's many grand buildings and mosques. Some of this stone was taken right off the Great Pyramid.

STRIKING DOWN THE ENEMY
There are only two known images of Khufu, builder of the Great Pyramid. One is a tiny ivory statue (p. 18). The other is this carving cut into a cliff in the Sinai Desert. It shows Khufu killing a Bedouin chieftain with a club. Thoth, the ibis-headed god of scribes, is looking on.

THE LAST WONDER
The three Giza pyramids were the oldest of the Seven Wonders of the Ancient World. But they are the only one left. The other six – the Lighthouse of Alexandria (right), the Colossus of Rhodes, the Hanging Gardens of Babylon, the Temple of Artemis, the Mausoleum at Halicarnassus, and the Statue of Zeus – are all vanished or in ruins.

One of three small queens' pyramids

Inside the pyramid

WHAT WONDERS ARE HIDDEN inside the pyramids? This question has fascinated people throughout history. The early Christians thought the pharaoh used them to store grain, as told in the story of Joseph in the Bible. But the pyramids were really royal tombs. Somewhere inside or beneath the huge mass of stone was a burial chamber where the dead king was laid to rest. Since the earliest times, there have been fantastic rumours about the glittering treasures buried with the dead pharaohs. To stop robbers, the pyramid builders hid the entrances and sealed the internal passages with huge plugs of stone. The Middle Kingdom kings created extra passages and false shafts to try and fool robbers. Despite all these efforts, every known pyramid had been looted by 1000 B.C. The few fragments that have been found were overlooked by hasty thieves. The only intact king's burial ever found belonged to Tutankhamun, who had been buried in a rock-cut tomb in the Valley of the Kings. He was lying in three stunning coffins, one made of solid gold, surrounded by price-less treasures. We can only imagine what marvels were buried inside the pyramids.

FORCED ENTRY
The original entrance to the Great Pyramid was concealed by polished casing blocks. Today visitors enter by a lower hole cut by the Arab leader Caliph Ma'mun in the 9th century.

EXPLORING WITHIN
In 1818, the famous Italian adventurer Giovanni Belzoni became the first European to enter Khafra's pyramid at Giza. He was disappointed to find that the burial chamber had been thoroughly robbed. The massive granite sarcophagus was still set into the floor. But there was no trace of the king's body or any treasures.

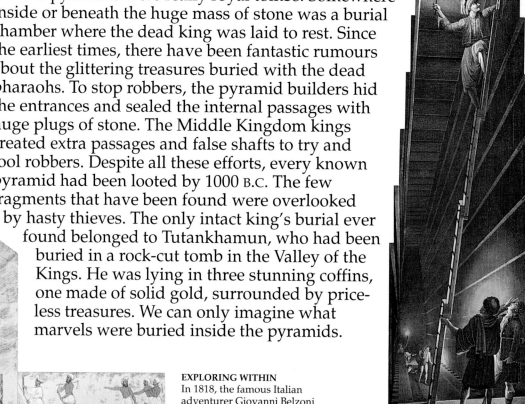

Two views of French explorers in the Grand Gallery of the Great Pyramid, from the *Description of Egypt*, 1809–1822.

STARS ON THE CEILING
The burial chamber was at the very heart of the pyramid. The sarcophagus often sat at the far end. The roof followed the angle of the pyramid. Unas's pyramid is decorated with stars and hieroglyphs.

Texts from Unas's pyramid

Stars from roof

Painted decoration

The Pyramid Texts

On the inner walls of King Unas's pyramid are the earliest known religious hieroglyphs. These are the Pyramid Texts. Once brightly coloured, these magical spells, prayers, and hymns are about the rebirth of the king and his reunion with the gods in the afterlife. They date from about 2340 B.C., which makes them the oldest known religious writings. Later versions of the texts were painted on Middle Kingdom coffins, and on New Kingdom papyruses, in the famous Book of the Dead.

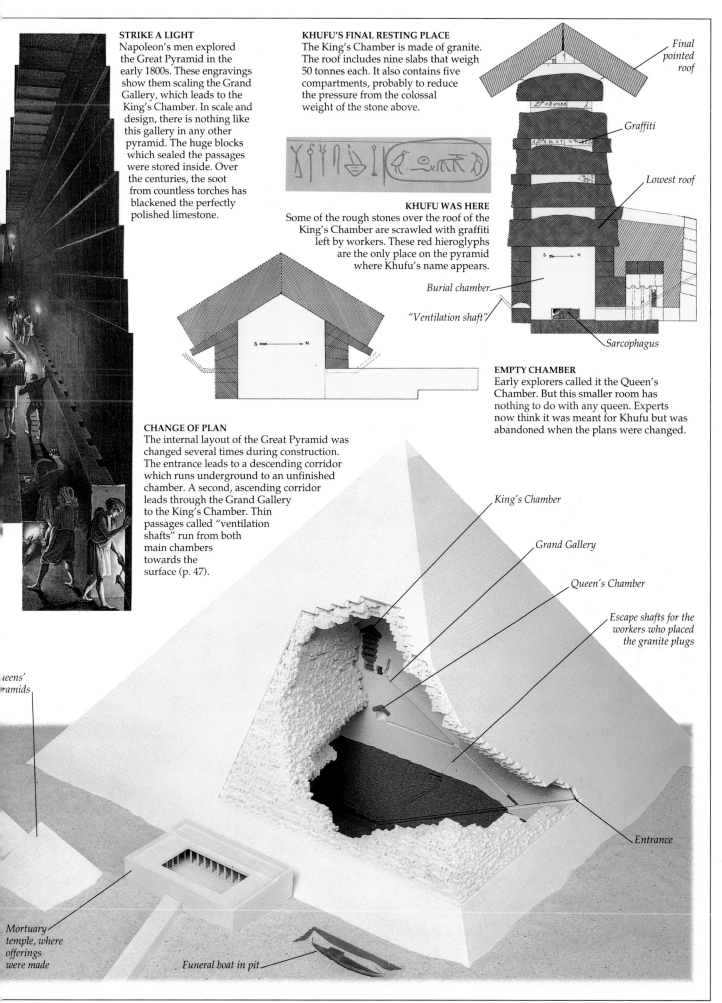

STRIKE A LIGHT
Napoleon's men explored the Great Pyramid in the early 1800s. These engravings show them scaling the Grand Gallery, which leads to the King's Chamber. In scale and design, there is nothing like this gallery in any other pyramid. The huge blocks which sealed the passages were stored inside. Over the centuries, the soot from countless torches has blackened the perfectly polished limestone.

KHUFU'S FINAL RESTING PLACE
The King's Chamber is made of granite. The roof includes nine slabs that weigh 50 tonnes each. It also contains five compartments, probably to reduce the pressure from the colossal weight of the stone above.

KHUFU WAS HERE
Some of the rough stones over the roof of the King's Chamber are scrawled with graffiti left by workers. These red hieroglyphs are the only place on the pyramid where Khufu's name appears.

Final pointed roof

Graffiti

Lowest roof

Burial chamber

"Ventilation shaft"

Sarcophagus

S → N

EMPTY CHAMBER
Early explorers called it the Queen's Chamber. But this smaller room has nothing to do with any queen. Experts now think it was meant for Khufu but was abandoned when the plans were changed.

CHANGE OF PLAN
The internal layout of the Great Pyramid was changed several times during construction. The entrance leads to a descending corridor which runs underground to an unfinished chamber. A second, ascending corridor leads through the Grand Gallery to the King's Chamber. Thin passages called "ventilation shafts" run from both main chambers towards the surface (p. 47).

King's Chamber

Grand Gallery

Queen's Chamber

Escape shafts for the workers who placed the granite plugs

Entrance

Queens' pyramids

Mortuary temple, where offerings were made

Funeral boat in pit

Temples and offerings

A TYPICAL PYRAMID COMPLEX included two temples connected by a long causeway. After the king died, his body was rowed across the Nile to the river or valley temple. Here it was mummified – embalme anointed with oils, and wrapped in linen bandages. Seventy days late the funeral began. Priests led the procession, while women wailed an threw sand into the air. The dead king was carried up the causeway to the mortuary or offering temple next to the pyramid. Here the priests performed sacred rites on the mummy before it was laid to rest in the pyramid. After the burial, the pharaoh's spirit would need regular supplies of food and drink. Every day, meals were placed on an altar in the mortuary temple. Before he died, the king would have set aside lands for the maintenance of a community of priests. Their duty was to maintain the temple and provide offerings for the dead king long into the future.

PEEK-A-BOO
This is a statue of Ti, an important official in charge of worship at the pyramid temples of Abusir (pp. 38–39). It was meant as a substitute body that Ti's spirit could inhabit after his death. The statue was placed in a special dark chamber in his tomb called a *serdab*, from the Arabic word for cellar. Ti's face could peer out of a spy hole cut into the tomb wall.

IN THE SHADOW OF THE GREAT PYRAMID
The Great Pyramid was surrounded by a mass of smaller buildings. Khufu's mortuary temple was built on the east side, where the sun was reborn (rose) every day. The dead king hoped to be reborn in the same way. The temple centred around an oblong court with 50 red granite columns. The contrast of white limestone walls, a black basalt floor, and red columns must have been very beautiful. Unfortunately the temple was destroyed long ago. This picture shows the tomb of the nobleman Seshemnufer. Like many important Egyptians, he chose to be buried in the shadow of Khufu's monstrous tomb.

LAND OF PLENTY
The spirits of the dead depended upon the living for their survival i the next world. Tomb pictures ofte show heaps of bread, beer, fruit, vegetables, and geese piled high on table. By reciting the formula writte beside it, the dead person could ha a fantastic banquet in the afterlife

Tomb entrance

Statues of Seshemnufer

MAGIC DOORWAY
...ourful images of food and drink decorate the
...se door of Prince Merib. If no offerings were
...eft, these magic pictures would come to life.

ESTATE MANAGER
The dead person's
family was often
pictured on the walls
of the tomb. These two
young women holding
ointment jars are the daughters
of Sennedjsui, a treasurer to the king
around 2150 B.C. He ran an estate where
food for offerings was grown. His titles
included "Sole Friend of the King".

ANCIENT BOOK-KEEPING
Scribes at the pyramid temple of
Neferirkara (p. 38) kept a detailed
record of all offerings. These
fragments are among the
earliest known writings
on papyrus. They list
daily deliveries of
food, including
joints of meat,
bread, and beer.

...alse doors and stelae

...orshippers came to pray and lay offerings before a stela or false
...oor in the mortuary temple. The stela was a slab of stone inscribed
...ith the dead person's name and titles. In the Old Kingdom, it often
...ok the form of a false door connecting the world of the living with
...e world of the dead. The door did not open. But the dead person's
... (spirit) was thought to pass through it, so he or she could leave
...e tomb and enjoy a meal in the temple.

Magic hieroglyphs

*Falcons represent
the high quality
of the cloth*

*The stela would
have been set up in
the eastern face of
Nefertiabet's tomb*

Leopard-skin robe

...AILY BREAD
...incess Nefertiabet
...as buried in a tomb at
...za. She was probably
...daughter of one of the
...araohs who built their
...ramids there. Her
...ela shows the princess
...earing the leopard-skin
...be of a priest. She is
...ated at a table piled
...gh with loaves of sacred
...ead. A leg of meat and
...headless goose hover
...ove the table. On the
...ght is a list of precious
...en to clothe the
...incess in the afterlife.

The Great Sphinx

Winged sphinx
made of ivory

FOR MORE THAN 4,500 YEARS, the Sphinx has guarded Khafra's pyramid at Giza. Carved from a huge outcrop of limestone, it is the largest free-standing sculpture to survive from ancient times. It has the body of a lion and the head of a king. The drifting sands have buried it up to the neck for most of its history. Attempts were made to clear it as early as 1400 B.C., by Thutmosis IV. When he was a prince, Thutmosis fell asleep under the Sphinx's head after a tiring hunt in the desert. In the prince's dream, the Sphinx promised to make him king if he freed it from the suffocating sand. After he had dug the Sphinx out, the prince recorded his dream on a stone tablet between its huge paws.

HEADS LIKE RAMS
In later times, the sphinx became popular as an image of Amun, the most important state god. A long avenue lined with ram-headed sphinxes once linked the great temples of Karnak and Luxor. This pair of bronze sphinxes comes from Nubia (pp. 48–53).

THE SPHINX'S BEARD
This fragment of the Sphinx's beard was found in the sand beneath its head. The beard was probably added a thousand years after the Sphinx was built. Its surface still has traces of its original red colouring. It seems to have been held in place by a column of stone that included a colossal statue of a pharaoh.

BATTERED AND WORN
The Sphinx was carved from an outcrop of rock that was too crumbly to be cut into building blocks for Khafra's pyramid. Its shape probably suggested the form of a lion, onto which Khafra's stone masons carved an image of their king. The sculpture is about 57 m (187 ft) long and 20 m (66 ft) high. The limestone has been badly weathered over the centuries. The paws were protected with stone facings in Roman times. These were redone recently.

Stone facings added to protect paws

GUARDING THE PYRAMID
Statues of lions often guard the entrances to Egyptian temples. The Sphinx was probably meant to protect the pyramid complex of Khafra in the same way. There is no evidence that it was worshipped in its own right when the pyramids were built. But in later times the Sphinx was identified with Horemakhet, or "Horus in the horizon", a form of the sun god.

e sculpture is wearing
nemes headcloth, a
mbol of royalty

The Sphinx stands next to the causeway of Khafra's pyramid, looking east towards the rising sun

In the 15th century A.D., Muslim troops smashed off the Sphinx's nose because their religion forbids images of a god

Crumbling limestone, eroded by blowing sand and pollution

BURIED IN THE DRIFTING SANDS
In 1818, an Italian sea captain, Giovanni Caviglia, tried to find a way into the Sphinx. He cleared the sand off its chest and uncovered a chapel. This was one of many modern attempts to free the Sphinx from the desert sands. It was finally dug out in 1925. Many conservationists are worried about the effects of pollution on its crumbling body. Some even suggest it may be safer buried in the sand again!

Stone stela (tablet) erected by Thutmosis IV to record his dream

Funeral boats

BOATS WERE THE most important means of transport for ancient Egyptians. They had no wheeled vehicles or major roads – their only highway was the Nile. In their religion, the Egyptians believed that the sun god Re sailed across the sky in a boat (p. 45). While the pharaoh was alive, he travelled the Nile and took part in state occasions in a beautiful boat. When he died, the pharaoh needed a boat in the land of the dead. In the Old and Middle Kingdoms, real boats were sometimes buried in pits next to a pharaoh's pyramid. The most famous boat belonged to King Khufu, builder of the Great Pyramid. It is massive, 43.5 m (143 ft) long. In later periods, small models of boats were placed in tombs instead.

SHIP SHAPE
In 1895, two wooden boats were foun in a pit near the pyramid of Senusret (p. 42). Most of the boat pits that have been excavated were empty. Th Egyptians may have believed that th dug-out shape provided a magical substitute for a real boat.

3,800 YEAR-OLD OAR
The Egyptians did not have rudders on their boats. Instead they steered with long oars mounted at the stern (back) of the boat. This is a steering oar found with one of the funeral boats of Senusret III. It dates from the Middle Kingdom, around 1850 B.C.

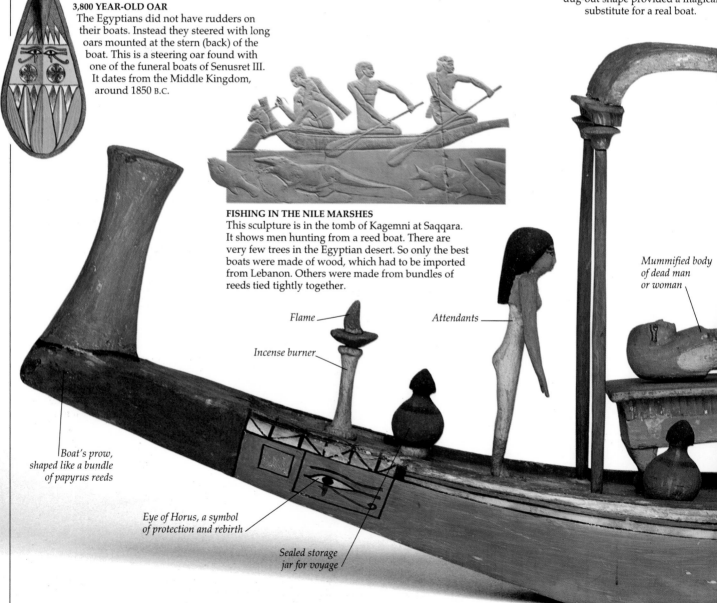

FISHING IN THE NILE MARSHES
This sculpture is in the tomb of Kagemni at Saqqara. It shows men hunting from a reed boat. There are very few trees in the Egyptian desert. So only the best boats were made of wood, which had to be imported from Lebanon. Others were made from bundles of reeds tied tightly together.

Mummified body of dead man or woman

Flame

Incense burner

Attendants

Boat's prow, shaped like a bundle of papyrus reeds

Eye of Horus, a symbol of protection and rebirth

Sealed storage jar for voyage

FUNERAL PROCESSION

Book of the Dead is a series of spells to help dead person's soul in the journey through the afterlife. This detail from the book by the scribe Hunefer shows a funeral procession. The mummy of Hunefer is carried in a boat mounted on a sledge pulled by priests. At the front of the procession, mourners wail and throw sand in the air.

Khufu's funeral boat

In 1954, an Egyptian archaeologist made a remarkable discovery. Just south of the Great Pyramid of Giza, he discovered a boat pit sealed for over 4,500 years. Under massive slabs of limestone lay 651 pieces of carved timber. These were put together to make an elegant boat. The name of King Khufu, builder of the Great Pyramid, was written on some of the pieces. It must have been buried by his successor, Radjedef, right after Khufu's death.

Khufu's boat on display in a museum next to the Great Pyramid

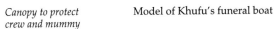

Prow shaped like bundle of reeds

Five pairs of oars

Canopy

The royal cabin

Stern

Steering oar

Model of Khufu's funeral boat

BOAT BENEATH THE PYRAMID

Khufu's boat had been dismantled to fit it into the pit. Luckily the builders had made notations such as "fore" and "aft" on some of the pieces. These clues helped the team who rebuilt the boat 4,500 years later. Tests on the wood show the boat was used at least once. This may have been while Khufu was alive, or to carry his body to the pyramid tomb during his funeral.

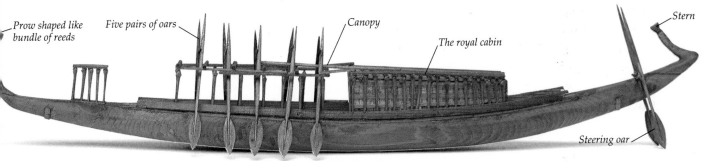

Canopy to protect crew and mummy from hot sun

Falcon heads

Steering oars

Steersman crouching at stern

Stern of carved wood shaped like a bundle of papyrus reeds

Priest with shaved head

Papyrus leaf decoration painted on blades

FUNERAL BOAT FROM THE MIDDLE KINGDOM

This model boat is carrying a mummy on a pilgrimage to Abydos. This sacred city was the centre of worship for the god Osiris, who was thought to have risen from the dead. All Egyptians hoped that their mummy would follow Osiris's example. The boat probably dates from the Middle Kingdom, 2055–1650 B.C. At that time small wooden boats were often placed in tombs, along with numerous objects, such as food, make-up, and furniture, that the dead person would need in the afterlife.

Planning the pyramid

THE PYRAMIDS REQUIRED careful planning. First a site had to be chosen. For religious reasons, this was always on the west bank of the Nile, where the sun set. It had to be close to the river, because the stone would arrive by boat, but well above flood level. The pyramid also required a solid base of rock that would not crack under its enormous weight. Then the site was leveled and true north was calculate so the sides could be lined up with the four compass points. The Egyptians probably did this by using the stars, since they did not have magnetic compasses. They had set squares and special tools like the *merkhet* to help in their calculations.

Pegging the foundations

DIVINE PROPORTIONS
Like sculpture and painting, pyramid building followed a fixed system of proportion. Artists' models like this one show that the Egyptians drew a grid of horizontal and vertical lines to calculate what they called "divine proportions". They used small models or sketches to plan large works. Two small limestone models of pyramids have been found. But there is no way of knowing if these were made before or after the pyramids.

LEVEL PEGGING
This ancient cord on a peg is probably one of a pair used to mark out the foundations of a building. The south-east corner of the Great Pyramid is only 1.3 cm (0.5 in) higher than the north-west corner. This incredible accuracy was achieved by digging trenches, filling them with water, and marking the level. Then all the rock above the line was hacked away until the foundation was perfectly flat.

Wooden peg

Cord made from the plant flax

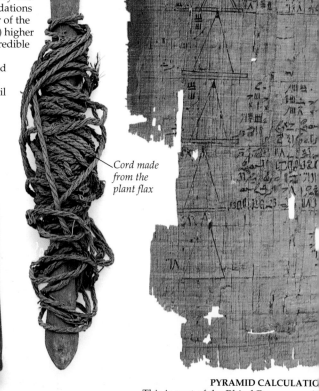

GUARANTEEING A TIGHT FIT
Egyptian masons had tools called boning rods to make the stone blocks perfectly smooth. This scene from the tomb of Rekhmire (c. 1450 B.C.) shows how these were used. The masons are holding the rods at right angles to the stone so the string is stretched tight. Any bumps are chiseled smooth.

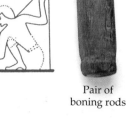

BREAKING THE RULES
The basic unit of measurement was the cubit, the length from the elbow to the tip of the thumb. This was equal to 52.4 cm (20.62 in). The wooden rod below is marked in cubits, palms, and digits. There were four digits in a palm, and seven palms in a cubit. The Egyptians also buried ritual cubit rods during foundation ceremonies.

Pair of boning rods

Fragment from a ritual cubit rod made of schist

PYRAMID CALCULATIO
This is part of the Rhind Papyrus, writ about 1650 B.C. It shows a series of proble about the relationship between the angle pyramid and its overall dimensions. The an of the sloping sides is called the *seked*. equal to half the width of the base, divided the pyramid's height and multiplied by sev

The scribe is wearing a double wig – his head may have been shaved underneath

This statue made of brown quartzite dates from about 700 B.C.

Cutting the earth

Pouring seed or incense

Moulding the first mud brick

...SSING THE FOUNDATIONS

...ding foundations had magical significance ...he Egyptians. These drawings show a pharaoh ...orming sacred rites at a foundation ceremony ...Edfu Temple. This is like the modern custom ...etting a famous person to lay the first brick.

Ink wells and palette slung over shoulder

WRITING IT DOWN
Scribes recorded the planning stages of the pyramid. On the building site, they kept notes of how much stone was used, and which tools each team was given. If a worker called in sick, the scribe wrote down his excuse.

Scribe is holding an unrolled papyrus scroll with his name, Pesshu-per, written on it in hieroglyphs

...EF OF SCRIBES
...sire's titles included "chief ...cribes" and "chief dentist". ...s picture of him dates from ...0 B.C., around the time the ...p Pyramid at Saqqara was ...t (pp. 10–13). He is shown ...h ink wells, a palette, and ...en case over his shoulder. ...holds a staff and sceptre, ...nbols of authority, and is ...ted at a table piled high ...h loaves of bread.

Scribes are usually shown sitting cross-legged

Hieroglyphic text to secure offerings to the gods for eternity

Building in brick and stone

It took hundreds of thousands of pieces of stone to build a pyramid. The Great Pyramid is made of about 2,300,000 blocks, weighing an average of 2.5 tonnes. The largest slabs, in the roof of the King's Chamber, weigh 50 tonnes. Quarrying all this stone and moving it to the site was an awesome task. The core of the pyramid was made from local limestone, a fairly soft rock. But the high-quality limestone used for the outer casing came from Tura, across the Nile. Some internal chambers and passages were made of granite, a harder stone that came from Aswan, 800 km (500 miles) upriver. All year round, gangs of workers at the quarries cut rough stone blocks out of the ground. When the river flooded and rose closer to the quarries, the stone blocks were loaded onto boats and carried to the pyramid site. The teams even wrote their names on the stones – some blocks in the Meidum Pyramid are labelled "Boat Gang", "Enduring Gang", or "Vigorous Gang".

BASALT
This hard black stone could be highly polished. This made it popular for sarcophagi, sculpture, and monumental inscriptions like the Rosetta Stone.

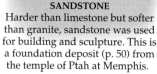

Both cartouches (royal names) of Ramses II, who ruled from 1279 to 1213 B.C.

SANDSTONE
Harder than limestone but softer than granite, sandstone was used for building and sculpture. This is a foundation deposit (p. 50) from the temple of Ptah at Memphis.

GRANITE
This hard, heavy stone was used for sculpture and sarcophagi (stone coffins) and sometimes for lining passages and chambers inside pyramids. It was very difficult to quarry. An unfinished obelisk is still lying in the Aswan quarry. It weighs over 1,000 tonnes and would have stood 30 m (100 ft) tall.

ROWING STONES
Quarries and pyramids were close to the Nile, so the stone could be transported by boat. This carving from the tomb of the official Ipi shows a cargo boat carrying a huge block of stone. The sail is rolled up, so the boat is probably cruising downstream (northwards) with the current.

RESTORATION PROJECT
The best Tura limestone was saved for the pyramid's outer casing. Most of these "casing blocks" were stripped away by later builders who were too lazy to quarry their own. This block shows the original angle of the pyramid of Unas at Saqqara, c. 2345 B.C., which has collapsed into a heap of rubble. More than a thousand years after it was built, Khaem-waset, Ramses II's son, tried to restore it by refitting the fallen casing blocks.

LIMESTONE
Old Kingdom pyramids were mostly made of limestone. Because papyrus – the ancient Egyptians' paper – was so expensive, sketches and rough notes were often done on fragments of pottery or limestone. These are called ostraca. This ostracon has a sketch of the god Osiris.

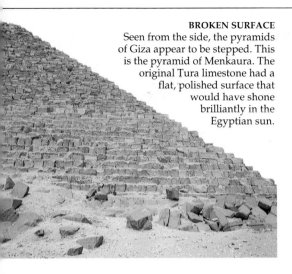

BROKEN SURFACE
Seen from the side, the pyramids of Giza appear to be stepped. This is the pyramid of Menkaura. The original Tura limestone had a flat, polished surface that would have shone brilliantly in the Egyptian sun.

BRICKMAKERS AT WORK
This painting from the tomb of Rekhmire at Thebes, c. 1450 B.C., shows workers mixing and moulding mud bricks.

Straw and sand keep the brick from cracking when it dries

Cartouche

1752

1931
6·13
9

ROYAL STAMP
Mud bricks were often stamped with the name of the pharaoh. This wooden stamp has the cartouche of King Amenhotep II, c. 1400 B.C.

Mud bricks

These were the most common building material in ancient Egypt. Middle Kingdom pyramids were made of mud bricks with only an outer facing of limestone. Today mud bricks are still made by the same process used by the ancients. Wet Nile mud is mixed with straw and sand and pushed into a wooden mould. Then the soft bricks are set out to dry in the burning sun. The Egyptian word for brick, *tobe,* is the origin of the modern word *adobe,* a kind of brick architecture.

Mud brick from Thebes, c. 1000 B.C.

A worker leaves rows of bricks to dry in the sun, in this picture from the tomb of Rekhmire

Tools for building

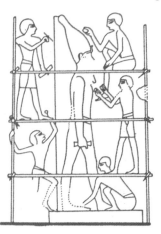

ROCK DRILL
This curved flake of flint is an Egyptian tool from the Pyramid Age. It looks too fragile to work stone. But attached to a wooden pole and spun vigorously with a bow, it became a powerful drill. For a smoother cut, the drill would be used with sand or crushed quartz, mixed with water or a little olive oil.

ALL AROUND THE GREAT temples, tombs, and pyramids, Egyptologists have found tools left by builders and sculptors. Some of these were lost or broken on the site. But others were left there for religious reasons. The Egyptians believed that a sacred building such as a temple or pyramid had a spirit that would have to be repaired in the next world. So the workers left tools for their spirits to use after they died. The design of these tools has barely changed over the centuries. It is amazing what wonders the builders created with such simple implements.

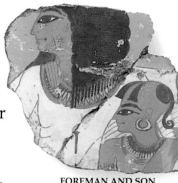

FOREMAN AND SON
Tools were precious. They were ofte issued each morning by a foreman who organized his team of worker and locked the tools away at night. T painting shows Anherkhau, a forem who worked in the Valley of the Kin with his son. It dates from 1150 B.C

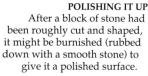

HIGHER AND HIGHER
Ancient paintings show that the Egyptians built scaffolding. This detail from the tomb of Rekhmire, c. 1450 B.C., shows workers putting the final touches on a statue of the pharaoh. They are standing on a network of light poles lashed together with knots of plant rope.

POLISHING IT UP
After a block of stone had been roughly cut and shaped, it might be burnished (rubbed down with a smooth stone) to give it a polished surface.

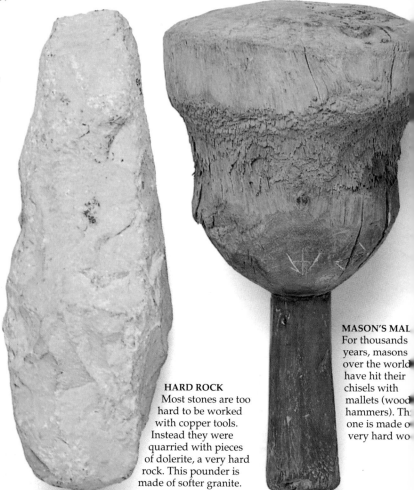

MASON'S MAL
For thousands years, masons over the world have hit their chisels with mallets (wood hammers). Th one is made o very hard wo

HARD ROCK
Most stones are too hard to be worked with copper tools. Instead they were quarried with pieces of dolerite, a very hard rock. This pounder is made of softer granite.

Copper

Bronze

CHISELS
Masons work stone with chisels. These bronze and copper chisels were used to create fine details. The tips could be heated to make them cut better.

Wide "dovetail" end was pushed into a recess in the stone and stuck there with plaster or mortar

BUTTERFLY CLAM
Clamps were used to hold blocks of stone together. Th wide ends were plastered into hol in the two stones. Many clamps are inscribed with the cartouche (name) the royal builder.

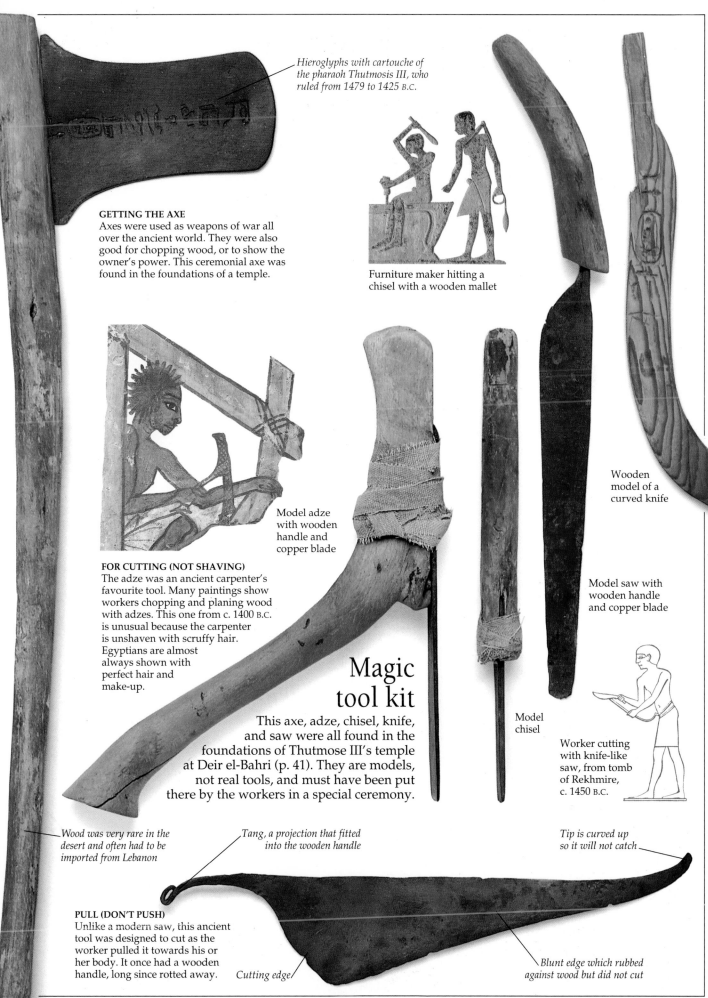

GETTING THE AXE
Axes were used as weapons of war all over the ancient world. They were also good for chopping wood, or to show the owner's power. This ceremonial axe was found in the foundations of a temple.

Hieroglyphs with cartouche of the pharaoh Thutmosis III, who ruled from 1479 to 1425 B.C.

Furniture maker hitting a chisel with a wooden mallet

Wooden model of a curved knife

FOR CUTTING (NOT SHAVING)
The adze was an ancient carpenter's favourite tool. Many paintings show workers chopping and planing wood with adzes. This one from c. 1400 B.C. is unusual because the carpenter is unshaven with scruffy hair. Egyptians are almost always shown with perfect hair and make-up.

Model adze with wooden handle and copper blade

Model saw with wooden handle and copper blade

Model chisel

Magic tool kit
This axe, adze, chisel, knife, and saw were all found in the foundations of Thutmose III's temple at Deir el-Bahri (p. 41). They are models, not real tools, and must have been put there by the workers in a special ceremony.

Worker cutting with knife-like saw, from tomb of Rekhmire, c. 1450 B.C.

Wood was very rare in the desert and often had to be imported from Lebanon

Tang, a projection that fitted into the wooden handle

Tip is curved up so it will not catch

PULL (DON'T PUSH)
Unlike a modern saw, this ancient tool was designed to cut as the worker pulled it towards his or her body. It once had a wooden handle, long since rotted away.

Cutting edge

Blunt edge which rubbed against wood but did not cut

The pyramid rises

No records survive to tell us how the pyramids were built. The only ancient account, by the Greek historian Herodotus, was written 2,000 years later and cannot be trusted. He claimed that gangs of 100,000 workmen toiled for 20 years to build the Great Pyramid. We now believe that about 4,000 skilled labourers worked all year round. This number was swelled during *Akhet*, the yearly flood, which lasted for about three months. Then thousands of peasants left their flooded fields and came to help on the site. There are many theories about how the heavy blocks of stone were lifted into place. Herodotus said they used lifting machines, but there is no evidence for this. It seems more likely that the stones were dragged up a ramp that grew as the pyramid rose.

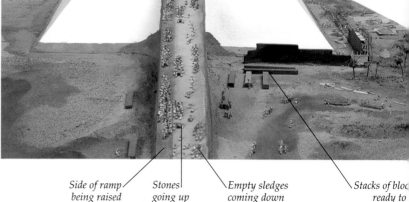

MUD-BRICK RAM
Remains of ramps have been found ne several pyramids. This detailed drawing from the tomb of Rekhmire, made 1,0 years after the Great Pyramid. It sho a building block lying on a ram

TWO-WAY TRAFFIC
The ramp was probably strictly organized into up and down lanes. One lane – in this model, the far left lane – is being raised, and is closed to traffic.

BUILDING A TRUE PYRAMID
This model shows the most popular theory – the use of one long supply ramp. As the pyramid grew higher, the ramp was increased in height and length. The top of the pyramid was a great square platform ready to receive the next layer of stones. In the model, the fine outer casing stones are being added as each layer is finished. But some experts argue that the whole pyramid was cased from the top down at the end. The boat is delivering logs for use in ramps, rollers, and scaffolding.

Polis casing probo w

Side of ramp being raised

Stones going up

Empty sledges coming down

Stacks of bloc ready to hauled up ram

The ramp was quite narrow, and was always kept at a gentle angle

Teams of men, at least 30 per sledge, pull stones up ramp

BIG DRAG

Wooden sledges with runners were the best way of moving heavy loads. Sledges are quite common in Egyptian art, and several real sledges have been found. This papyrus painting (c.1000 B.C.) shows a funeral procession. Men are dragging the coffin, which is covered by a canopy and mounted on a sledge. When moving stones, the workers probably laid logs across the ramp to stop the heavy sledges from getting bogged down in the mud.

UPWARD SPIRAL

Some experts have proposed that the stones were dragged up a system of spiral ramps winding around the pyramid. These could have stood on the casing blocks, or on separate foundations in front of the pyramid. But it would have been virtually impossible to turn the stones around the corners. Spiral ramps would also obscure the whole pyramid, which would make measurements difficult. Making sure the four sides came to a perfect point would have required constant measuring.

CRACK THE WHIP

Romantic drawings and films often show sweating slaves being driven on by bosses with whips. This is totally untrue. The hard labour was done by peasant farmers. They believed their pharaoh was a god, and were probably happy to help him achieve everlasting life.

...rkers add to ...ght of ramp

A team dragging a block of stone arrives at the top

Awnings to shelter foremen and supplies of food and water

Fine white Tura limestone for outer casing

Stockpile of local limestone for core

Teams work on scaffolding to fit the final casing stones on each layer

Work in progress on entrance to internal passages in north face of pyramid

As the wall gets higher, the workers use wooden pole scaffolding

Teams of workmen build the square enclosure wall which will run right around the pyramid

A slow decline

THE KINGS OF EGYPT'S fifth and sixth dynasties continued the tradition of pyramid building. But their pyramids were smaller and not as well built. The largest, made for King Neferirkara at Abusir, is about the same size as Menkaura's pyramid, the smallest of the Giza trio. The kings still cased their pyramids in fine Tura limestone. But underneath was a core of small, roughly joined stones. These have slowly collapsed, so that little more than piles of rubble remain. The cult of the sun god increased during this period, and many sun temples were built. These magnificent buildings were places of worship and centres for food offerings, which were taken by boat and placed in nearby pyramid temples.

EASY ACCESS
The fifth and sixth dynasty kings did not make much effort to conceal the entrances to their pyramids. This made it easy for tomb robbers to get in. This drawing shows the entrance to Nyuserra's pyramid at Abusir. It comes from Howard Vyse's famous book *The Pyramids of Gizeh,* published in 1837.

MAGIC HIEROGLYPHS
Magic spells were essential to guaran the king's survival in the afterlife. The hieroglyphs from the pyramid temple King Sahura state his many royal title

Falcon

The king is holding the divine mace, a weapon and symbol of royal power

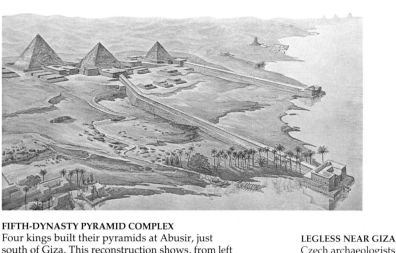

FIFTH-DYNASTY PYRAMID COMPLEX
Four kings built their pyramids at Abusir, just south of Giza. This reconstruction shows, from left to right, the pyramids of Neferirkara, Nyuserra, and Sahura. Beyond them are the sun temples of Userkaf and Nyuserra. The causeway (raised approach) to Nyuserra's pyramid takes a sharp turn, because it was originally meant to lead to the pyramid of the earlier king Neferirkara. After his death, the king was mummified in or around the river temple. Then his mummy was carried up the causeway, and sacred rites were performed in the pyramid temple. Finally the dead king was laid to rest beneath the pyramid.

LEGLESS NEAR GIZA
Czech archaeologists identified the ruined pyramid of Raneferef in 1982. It is in Abusir and dates from about 2445 B.C. This beautiful statue of the king was found in his mortuary temple. Behind his head is a falcon, a symbol of royalty and the god Horus. It clasps *shenu* rings, which symbolize eternity, in its claws. The king was once sitting down, but his legs have been broken off.

Statue is carved from pink limestone

The top of the king's kilt

ENDURANCE TEST
Despite its name, "The places of Nyuserra are enduring", this pyramid is just a pile of sand and rubble.

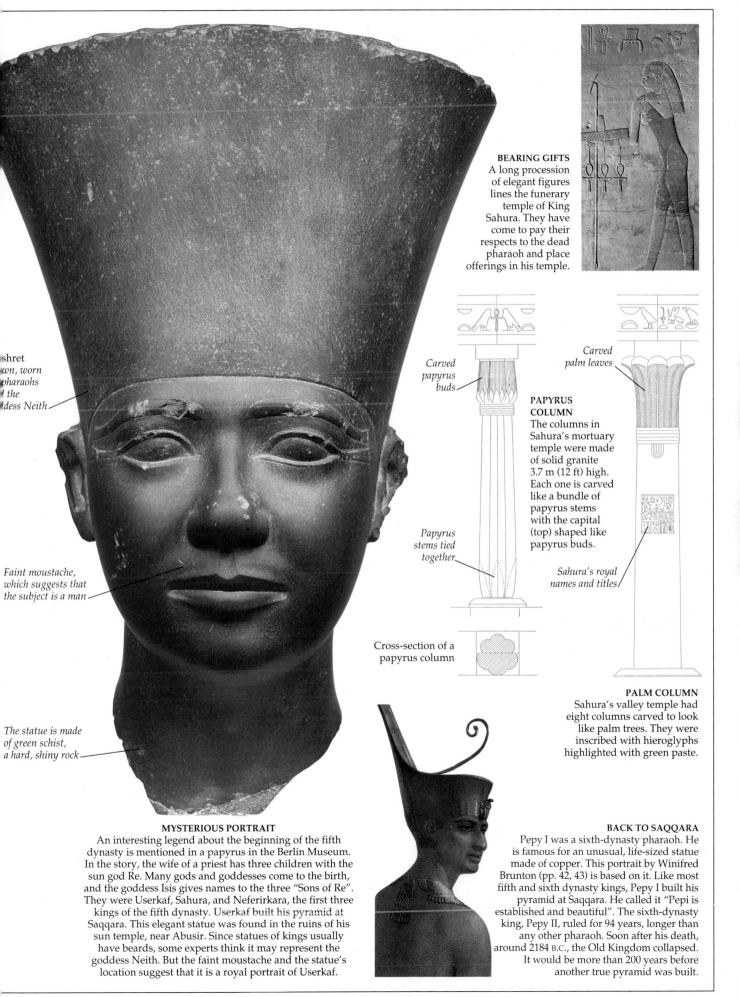

shret
...wn, worn
...pharaohs
... the
...dess Neith

Faint moustache,
which suggests that
the subject is a man

The statue is made
of green schist,
a hard, shiny rock

BEARING GIFTS
A long procession
of elegant figures
lines the funerary
temple of King
Sahura. They have
come to pay their
respects to the dead
pharaoh and place
offerings in his temple.

Carved
papyrus
buds

Carved
palm leaves

**PAPYRUS
COLUMN**
The columns in
Sahura's mortuary
temple were made
of solid granite
3.7 m (12 ft) high.
Each one is carved
like a bundle of
papyrus stems
with the capital
(top) shaped like
papyrus buds.

Papyrus
stems tied
together

Sahura's royal
names and titles

Cross-section of a
papyrus column

PALM COLUMN
Sahura's valley temple had
eight columns carved to look
like palm trees. They were
inscribed with hieroglyphs
highlighted with green paste.

MYSTERIOUS PORTRAIT
An interesting legend about the beginning of the fifth
dynasty is mentioned in a papyrus in the Berlin Museum.
In the story, the wife of a priest has three children with the
sun god Re. Many gods and goddesses come to the birth,
and the goddess Isis gives names to the three "Sons of Re".
They were Userkaf, Sahura, and Neferirkara, the first three
kings of the fifth dynasty. Userkaf built his pyramid at
Saqqara. This elegant statue was found in the ruins of his
sun temple, near Abusir. Since statues of kings usually
have beards, some experts think it may represent the
goddess Neith. But the faint moustache and the statue's
location suggest that it is a royal portrait of Userkaf.

BACK TO SAQQARA
Pepy I was a sixth-dynasty pharaoh. He
is famous for an unusual, life-sized statue
made of copper. This portrait by Winifred
Brunton (pp. 42, 43) is based on it. Like most
fifth and sixth dynasty kings, Pepy I built his
pyramid at Saqqara. He called it "Pepi is
established and beautiful". The sixth-dynasty
king, Pepy II, ruled for 94 years, longer than
any other pharaoh. Soon after his death,
around 2184 B.C., the Old Kingdom collapsed.
It would be more than 200 years before
another true pyramid was built.

The Middle Kingdom revival

AFTER A LONG PERIOD OF DISORDER and civil war, Egypt was reunited around 2055 B.C. The period that followed is known as the Middle Kingdom. Strong kings expanded the empire and revived the tradition of pyramid building. They were inspired by the great pyramids of the Old Kingdom and often built their tombs near the old sites. But the Middle Kingdom pyramids do not have the same grandeur. They were usually based around a core of mud bricks, which has slowly collapsed over the years. Middle Kingdom pharaohs were preoccupied with creating complicated devices and false passages to stop thieves from finding their burial chambers. But the kings were buried with priceless treasures, and the robbers stopped at nothing. Despite the elaborate precautions, all the pyramids were robbed in the period of unrest that followed the end of the Middle Kingdom, around 1650 B.C.

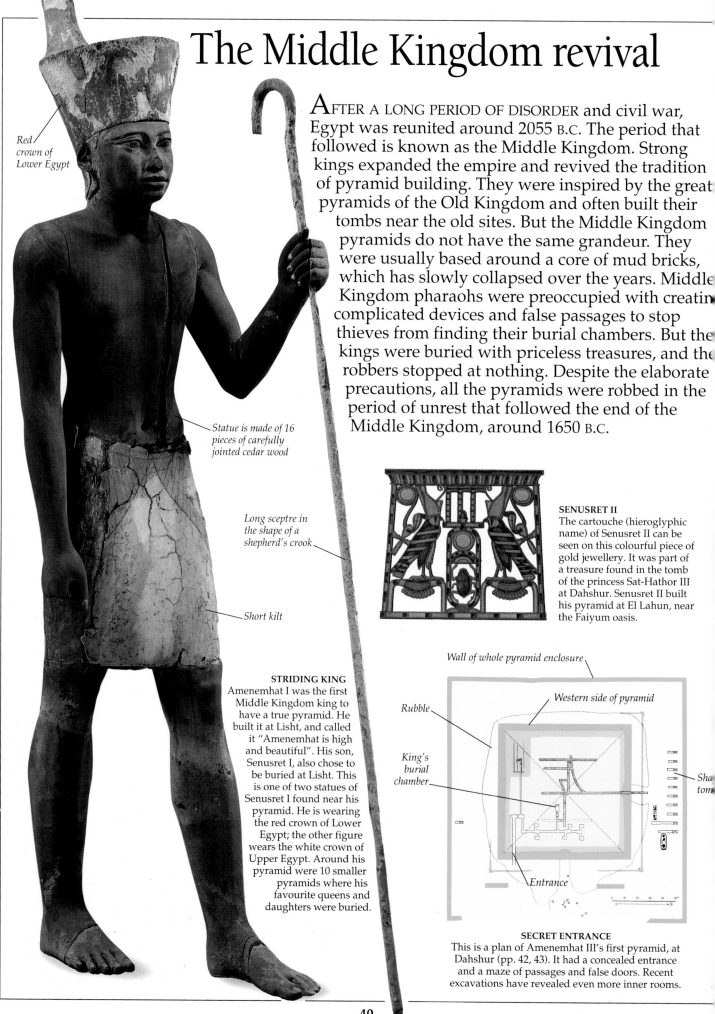

Red crown of Lower Egypt

Statue is made of 16 pieces of carefully jointed cedar wood

Long sceptre in the shape of a shepherd's crook

Short kilt

SENUSRET II
The cartouche (hieroglyphic name) of Senusret II can be seen on this colourful piece of gold jewellery. It was part of a treasure found in the tomb of the princess Sat-Hathor III at Dahshur. Senusret II built his pyramid at El Lahun, near the Faiyum oasis.

STRIDING KING
Amenemhat I was the first Middle Kingdom king to have a true pyramid. He built it at Lisht, and called it "Amenemhat is high and beautiful". His son, Senusret I, also chose to be buried at Lisht. This is one of two statues of Senusret I found near his pyramid. He is wearing the red crown of Lower Egypt; the other figure wears the white crown of Upper Egypt. Around his pyramid were 10 smaller pyramids where his favourite queens and daughters were buried.

Wall of whole pyramid enclosure

Western side of pyramid

Rubble

King's burial chamber

Sha tom

Entrance

SECRET ENTRANCE
This is a plan of Amenemhat III's first pyramid, at Dahshur (pp. 42, 43). It had a concealed entrance and a maze of passages and false doors. Recent excavations have revealed even more inner rooms.

Great temple at Deir el-Bahri

The first pharaoh of the Middle Kingdom, Nebhepetra Mentuhotep, was one of Egypt's greatest rulers. During his 51 years on the throne, art and architecture began to prosper again. Mentuhotep chose a bay in the cliffs at Deir el-Bahri, near Thebes, for his funerary temple. This unusual complex had colonnades, a ramp, and rows of statues and trees. High on a terrace were six shrines with shafts leading to the tombs of the king's wives and daughters. There were two more tombs beneath the temple, but Mentuhotep's mummy or coffin was not found in either one. The whole complex is badly preserved. It has been overshadowed by a similar, larger temple built 500 years later by Queen Hatshepsut.

OLY OF HOLIES
n her own era, Hatshepsut as famous for her radiant eauty. The ancient Egyptians alled her temple Djeseru-jeseru, "Holy of Holies".

QUEEN WITH A BEARD
Hatshepsut was one of the few women to be crowned pharaoh of Egypt. To strengthen her claim to the throne, she had herself portrayed as the daughter of the god Amun. This scene from Karnak temple shows her running in the royal *sed* course (pp. 12–13). She is wearing a false beard, a sign of royalty.

PYRAMID OR MASTABA?
Was Mentuhotep's temple capped with a stone pyramid? Until recently, most experts thought so. But a recent study suggested that the top storey may have been a flat-topped mastaba.

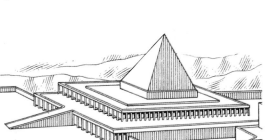

Red crown of Lower Egypt

Cobras, thought to protect the pharaoh by spitting fire at enemies

False beard, worn by the pharaoh on important occasions

EMBRACED BY A GODDESS
Mentuhotep reigned from 2055 to 2004 B.C. As a young king he re-united the two lands – Lower and Upper Egypt – and won many victories over the Nubians and Libyans. But unlike the great kings of the Old Kingdom, he did not make Memphis his capital. Instead he ruled from Thebes in the south (p. 8). In this fine fragment from Deir el-Bahri, he is shown being embraced by the hands of a goddess.

COLOURED RELIEF
The walls of Mentuhotep's temple at Deir el-Bahri were lined with colourful paintings. Thousands of broken fragments have been found in the ruins. They are now in museums all over the world. This fragment showing a man, probably an offering bearer, is in the Bolton Museum in England.

Continued on next page

FALCON PENDANT
This pendant is made of gold inlaid with the red stone cornelian. It is part of several magnificent treasures of jewellery found around the Middle Kingdom pyramids at Dahshur and El Lahun.

Senusret III

This great pharaoh reigned from 1874 to 1855 B.C. He created a strong, centralized government and conquered Nubia to the south. He built his pyramid at Dahshur. The design of the pyramid buildings and the king's sarcophagus was influenced by Djoser's Step Pyramid complex (pp. 10–13), built 800 years earlier.

Large ear featur many stat of this per

Ro ner headc

THE BLACK PYRAMID
Senusret III and his successor Amenemhat III built their pyramids at Dahshur, just south of Saqqara. This is Amenemhat III's pyramid, often called the Black Pyramid. Like most Middle Kingdom pyramids, it is now just a pile of rubble. The core of mud bricks has subsided over the centuries, and the fine stone facings were plundered for later building projects. The corridors and chambers, including the tombs of at least three queens, were dug about 12 m (40 ft) underground. But the king's burial chamber with its beautiful granite sarcophagus was never used.

PHARAOH'S FEATURES
This is Senusret III as he may have looked in life. It is one of a series of reconstructions of famous Egyptians painted by Winifred Brunton, based on careful observations of ancient statues.

Belt buckle w cartouche Senusret

Pleated k known a shendyt k

LOOKING HIS AGE
Senusret III looks stern and thoughtful in this statue carved from black granite. This new, more realistic style of portraiture was introduced during his reign.

The vulture goddess Nekhbet

Cartouche of Senusret III

A PRINCESS'S TREASURE
This beautiful piece of jewellery was found in the tomb of princess Mereret near the pyramid of Senusret III. One of the king's victories is symbolized by sphinxes trampling on Nubians.

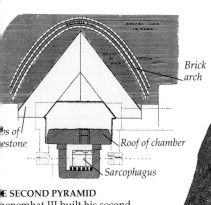

[TH]E SECOND PYRAMID
[Am]enemhat III built his second
[py]ramid at Hawara. His architects
[bui]lt an amazing series of devices
[to b]affle robbers – deep wells, blind
[cor]ridors, secret trap-doors, and
[pas]sages sealed with mighty stone
[slab]s. This is his burial chamber,
[wh]ich is covered by limestone
[blo]cks weighing 50 tonnes each.
[Thi]eves still broke in, stealing
[all] the king's treasures and
[bur]ning his body.

*Brick
arch*

Roof of chamber

Sarcophagus

[Re]construction painting of
[Am]enemhat III, by Winifred
[Bru]nton, done in the 1920s

MIGHTY HEAD
The eyes have been
gouged out of this massive
head of Amenemhat III. Carved
in black granite, it was once
part of a full-length statue.

Amenemhat III

The grandson of Senusret III, Amenemhat III was
one of the most powerful pharaohs ever to rule Egypt.
He built two pyramids and a famous labyrinth (maze)
said to contain 3,000 rooms. He is also credited with
building an impressive irrigation scheme. This was an
ancient forerunner of the Aswan Dam, with massive
dykes and sluices to control the water level of the Nile.

CAPSTONE
In the rubble around the
Dahshur pyramid, a granite
capstone was found. It is
carved with Amenemhat III's
royal titles and prayers to the
sun god. The hieroglyphs on
this detail read "Seeing the
beauty of Re". Why wasn't
Amenemhat buried in the
Dahshur pyramid? He may
have built it as a cenotaph, a
symbolic place for his spirit to
dwell. Or he may have decided
that the layout wasn't complex
enough to fool robbers.

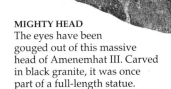

LORD OF ALL LANDS
Another piece of gold jewellery from Princess
Mereret's tomb. By Amenemhat III's cartouche
are hieroglyphs that read "The good god,
lord of all lands and foreign countries".

Pyramidions

THE MASSIVE ROYAL PYRAMIDS of old inspired private individuals to build pyramid-shaped tombs in the New Kingdom. These were small brick buildings with pointed roofs capped by a pyramidion, or capstone. They were often whitewashed and had stelae, stone tablets, on the front. Prayers to the sun god Re were inscribed on the stelae and pyramidions. A courtyard often stood in front of the tomb. This served as a chapel where worshippers could place offerings and pray. An underground passage led to a vaulted burial chamber where the mummy lay. Hundreds of these small pyramids were built on the west bank of the Nile by officials, scribes, and the artisans who worked on the great royal tombs of the New Kingdom.

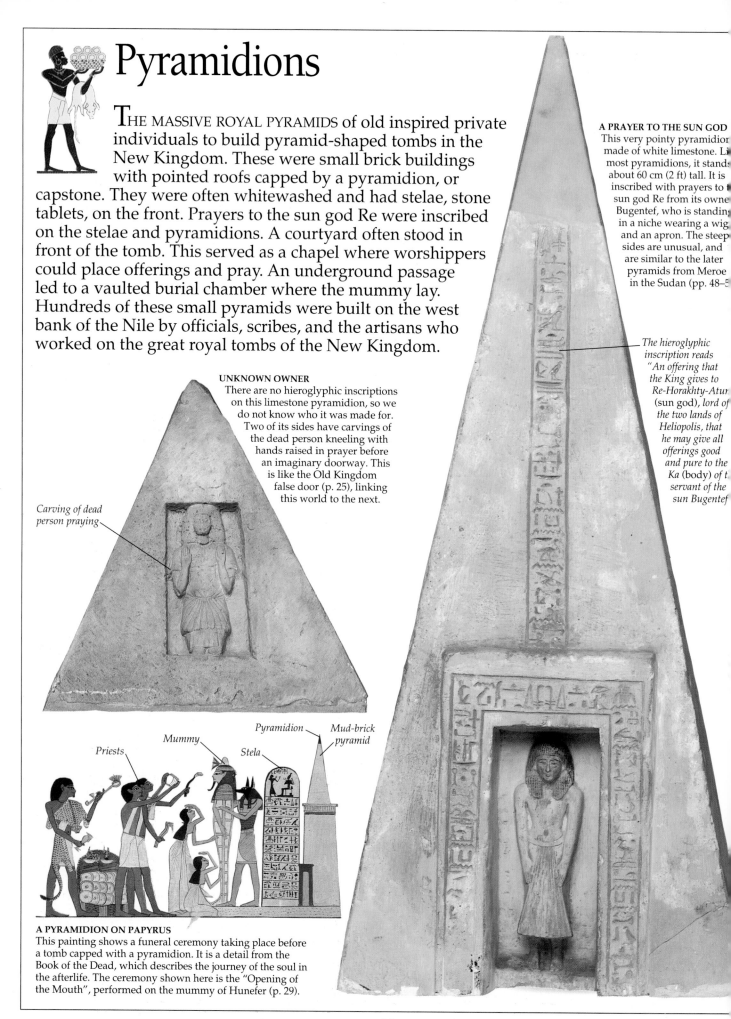

A PRAYER TO THE SUN GOD
This very pointy pyramidion made of white limestone. Li most pyramidions, it stands about 60 cm (2 ft) tall. It is inscribed with prayers to t sun god Re from its owne Bugentef, who is standing in a niche wearing a wig and an apron. The steep sides are unusual, and are similar to the later pyramids from Meroe in the Sudan (pp. 48–5)

The hieroglyphic inscription reads "An offering that the King gives to Re-Horakhty-Atun (sun god), lord of the two lands of Heliopolis, that he may give all offerings good and pure to the Ka (body) of t servant of the sun Bugentef

UNKNOWN OWNER
There are no hieroglyphic inscriptions on this limestone pyramidion, so we do not know who it was made for. Two of its sides have carvings of the dead person kneeling with hands raised in prayer before an imaginary doorway. This is like the Old Kingdom false door (p. 25), linking this world to the next.

Carving of dead person praying

Priests *Mummy* *Stela* *Pyramidion* *Mud-brick pyramid*

A PYRAMIDION ON PAPYRUS
This painting shows a funeral ceremony taking place before a tomb capped with a pyramidion. It is a detail from the Book of the Dead, which describes the journey of the soul in the afterlife. The ceremony shown here is the "Opening of the Mouth", performed on the mummy of Hunefer (p. 29).

...ubian captives carrying offerings,
...cluding fruits, beads, an elephant
...sk, and a leopard skin

...LING ACROSS THE SKY
...four sides of this pyramidion from
...B.C. are decorated with fine carving.
...s is the west side, dedicated to the
...god Re. The ancient Egyptians
...eved Re sailed across the heavens
...boat, rising in the east in the
...rning and setting in the west at
...end of the day. The south side
...tures Anubis performing rites
...the mummy of the dead
...n, Udjahor.

Anubis, god of the dead,
shown as a dog or jackal

...god Re, with the
...d of a falcon and a
...r disk on his head

...t to carry
...s and
...desses
...ough
...sky

SACRED SHAPE
This wall painting shows Nubians presenting
gifts and food offerings, including incense
in the sacred shape of a pyramid. Bread
was sometimes baked in pyramid-shaped
loaves. The Egyptians worshipped a sacred
stone at Heliopolis because they believed
that when the world was formed, the rays
of the rising sun had fallen on this stone
first of all. For this reason pyramidions
made of stone were also regarded as
dwelling places of the sun god.

Prayer to the
gods from the
dead person

Maat, the goddess of
law and order, with an
ostrich feather, a symbol
of truth, on her head

Udjahor, the
dead person,
worshipping

Riddles of the pyramids

Considering they were built 4,500 years ago, we know a surprising amount about the Egyptian pyramids. But many mysteries remain. Almost everything has been learned in the last two centuries. A great breakthrough was made in 1822, when the French scholar Jean-François Champollion began to decipher hieroglyphics, the Egyptian picture-writing. By then, the Egyptian language and civilization had been dead for nearly 2,000 years. The desert sands had swallowed up the smaller pyramids, and the names of the great kings and queens had been lost or forgotten. Modern archaeologists sift through these ruins, searching for tiny clues that will help them to piece together the puzzles of the past. The answers to some questions are still unclear. Exactly how were the pyramids built? And what is the religious significance of the shape? There are many theories, but we may never know for sure.

HOW MANY WORKERS DID IT TAKE?
Experts think it took 100,000 men 20 years to move all the sto for the Great Pyramid. Most of them were peasant farmers w worked on the pyramid only during the flood, which laste three months. Another 4,000 skilled workers were on the site year round. Their barracks have been found near the pyram

HOW MANY HAVEN'T BEEN DISCOVERED YET?
Some pyramids and pharaohs have only been discovered in the last few years. This gold shell comes from the so-called "Lost Pyramid" of Saqqara, which lay hidden under the desert sands until 1951. This unfinished tomb was built by Sekhemkhet, a pharaoh who was almost unknown until his name was found in the ruins. Who knows how many other pyramids still lie undiscovered beneath the shifting sands?

WERE THESE TOOLS USED TO BUILD THE GREAT PYRAMID
When Waynman Dixon discovered the mysterious "ventilati shafts" of the Queen's Chamber in the Great Pyramid (p. 23 he also found two small tools. They are a granite pounder and a metal hook. They may have been left there by workme No other tools used on the Giza pyramids have survived.

Colossal statue tied to a sledge with ropes *Man clapping to keep time* *Soldiers*

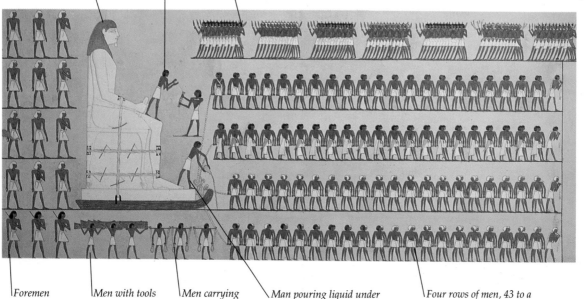

HOW DID THEY MOVE THE STONES?
There is no proof that the Egyptians used lifting machines, pulley or wheeled vehicles. But they definitely use sledges to move heavy objects. One of the best pieces of evidence is this drawing from the tomb of Djehutyhotep Bersha, from 1850 B.C. shows teams of worker dragging a huge stone statue. The Egyptians probably used similar methods to move and position the stones whe building the pyramids.

Foremen *Men with tools* *Men carrying water or grease* *Man pouring liquid under the sledge to grease its path* *Four rows of men, 43 to a row, dragging the statue*

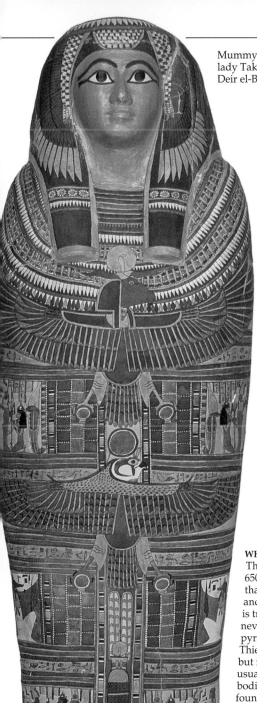

Mummy case of the
lady Takhenmes,
Deir el-Bahri, 700–650 B.C.

The constellation Orion,
including the three bright
stars of Orion's belt

Scottish astronomer
Charles Piazzi Smyth

Sun or stars?

There are all sorts of strange theories about the pyramids. Many of these try to explain the link with the sun and the stars. In 1864, for example, Piazzi Smyth claimed that the pyramids were built to God's measurements. Nowadays experts agree that the pyramid was a symbolic vehicle for sending the dead king's spirit to heaven. But was the king supposed to join the sun god Re, or become "an Indestructible Star"? The Pyramid Texts mention both. For instance, Spell 882 says "O king, thou art this great star, the companion of Orion". It is possible that step pyramids were part of a star cult, while true pyramids were associated with the sun. The "ventilation shafts" of the Great Pyramid may have been aligned with major stars like the Pole Star and Orion. But some experts think their use was purely practical.

WHERE ARE THE MUMMIES?

This is a mummy case from about 650 B.C. It has always been assumed that dead kings were mummified and buried in pyramids. But if this is true, why have human remains never been found inside a pyramid burial chamber? Thieves often steal treasures, but in other tombs they usually ignore the dead bodies. Until a mummy is found in a pyramid, the possibility that some kings were not buried inside cannot be ruled out. And if these pyramids are not tombs, what other religious function did they have?

Wood covered in gold

WHERE WAS QUEEN HETEPHERES BURIED?

The only intact royal burial from the Old Kingdom found so far belonged to Queen Hetepheres. She was Sneferu's wife and Khufu's mother. Her tomb had never been robbed, and included beautiful jewellery and furniture and the queen's embalmed organs. But the sarcophagus was empty. So where was the queen's body buried? Maybe at Dahshur, or in one of Khufu's queens' pyramids.

Reconstruction of a chair from the tomb of Queen Hetepheres at Giza, c. 2600 B.C.

Lion's paw legs

Pyramids of Nubia

To the south of Egypt further up the River Nile lies Nubia, know to the ancient Egyptians as "Kush". This desert land was one of the cradles of African civilization, and was rich in gold and exotic good Nubia's position on the Nile gave it great strategic importance, and for centuries Egypt's pharaohs fought to control it. There are more than a hundred pyramids in Nubia. They were all plundered for their stone over the centuries, and today most of them are shapeless mounds. Like the Egyptian pyramids, they were also robbed of their treasures long ago. The first Nubian pyramids were built around 700 B.C., during a brief period when the Nubian kings ruled Egypt. They are at Kurru and Nuri, near Napata, the Nubian capital. When the capital was moved south to Meroe, around 300 B.C., pyramids were also built there. The kings and queens were mummified and buried underneath. Servants were often sacrificed and buried in the pyramid too, so that they could wait on their kings and queens in the next world.

STEEP SIDES
Nubian pyramids are smaller than the great Egyptian ones and have much steeper sides. Against the eastern face was a small funerary chapel with a gateway decorated like an Egyptian temple. Priests and pilgrims who came to honour the dead king and queen said prayers and placed offerings within the chapel. This is one of the pyramids at Meroe, in modern Sudan, as it appeared in 1820. Some 14 years later, several pyramids at Meroe were badly damaged by an Italian adventurer searching for treasure (pp. 52–53).

God I

L
p

Ank
sign of

STEPPING DOWN
The burial chamber was dug under the pyramid, not built into the structure. It was approached by a long, descending flight of steps, which opened into a series of three connecting chambers cut deep into the bedrock.

GOOD LUCK CHARM
Some pyramids were built around Gebel Barkal. This strange, flat-topped peak was a sacred site for the Nubians, who called it "The Pure Mountain". This amulet was found there. It incorporates many magical symbols, including the ankh, the djed pillar, and a dog-headed sceptre. There is also a figure of the god Heh, who represented everlasting life.

Scep
symbo
power
domin

A PYRAMID FIELD AT MEROE
These are the pyramids in the northern cemetery at Meroe. They were built between 300 B.C. and about A.D. 350, when Nubia was conquered by the Axumites. By the first century A.D., Meroe was the centre of one of Africa's great civilizations. At its peak, Nubia was a fascinating mixture of Egyptian, Greek, Roman, and central African culture. As the kingdom declined, the kings built smaller, less impressive pyramids.

Two small, intact pyramids

The tops of the big pyram have been destro

Painted decoration of reeds
that runs around tomb

Log of ebony, an
extremely hard, black
tree that grows in the
Nubian desert

...ense

Lotuses,
sacred flowers
that still grow
by the Nile

Chunks of red
jasper, a precious
stone used in
jewellery

Leopard-skin kilt

EGYPTIAN STYLE
The Egyptians settled
in Nubia, founding new
towns and spreading their
culture. This faience pot is
decorated with lotus leaves
in a typical Egyptian style.

GIRAFFE TAILS FOR THE KING
Nubia was rich in natural
resources, especially gold. This
Egyptian tomb painting shows
Nubians giving exotic gifts to the
Egyptian pharaoh Thutmosis IV.
It was painted around 1400 B.C.

Live baboon

Gold rings

Giraffe tails

Leopard skin

Gateway with two
pylons leading to
small chapel

49

Pharaohs of Nubia

Around 750 B.C., when Egypt was weakened by civil wars and disorder, the Nubian kingdom prospered and grew powerful enough to conquer Egypt. For about a hundred years, the kings of Nubia were also pharaohs of Egypt. Succession to the throne was from brother to brother – not from father to son, the usual Egyptian practice. The Nubians were fascinated by the culture and religion of Egypt, and even restored temples there. They also adopted the Egyptian tradition of being buried with shabti figures. These mummy-shaped statues were thought to have magical powers to work for the dead person in the next world. The Egyptians were buried with 401 shabti figures – one for each day of the year, plus 36 bosses carrying whips. But one Nubian king had 1,277, more than three times the usual number.

Gold-covered cobra, worn on king's crown to spit fire at his enemies

Royal cobra

Nemes *headcloth, a sign of royalty*

Crossed hands holding farming tools

Cartouche of Anlamani

55510

55512

Cartouche (royal name) of Taharqo

Chapter six of the Book of the Dead

One of King Taharqo's 1,070 shabti figures, carved from translucent calcite

HEAVYWEIGHT KING
King Anlamani ruled before his brother, Aspelta. This shabti figure of the king is one of 282 found in his pyramid at Nuri. They were all carved by hand, not made in a mould. The king has a massive, chunky body, with a small head and a huge *nemes* headcloth. His shabti is inscribed with chapter six of the Book of the Dead, a spell telling it to do agricultural work in the next world.

NO BED
The best-preserved pyramid at Nuri belongs to King Aspelta. This is one of the 300 shabtis found inside. Aspelta was one of the first Nubian rulers to be buried in a coffin and a stone sarcophagus. Earlier kings were laid to rest in beds.

The great Taharqo

King Taharqo is the most famous Nubian king. He ruled over Nubia and Egypt from 690 to 664 B.C., at the height of the 25th dynasty. He is even mentioned in the Bible. Taharqo built many monuments and temples in both lands. His huge pyramid at Nuri was probably inspired by the great Giza pyramids, which he could see from his palace at Memphis.

MAGIC TABLETS
These are foundation deposits with the names of kings written on them. After a ritual ceremony, they were placed in the foundations at the four corners of the king's pyramid, to help it last forever.

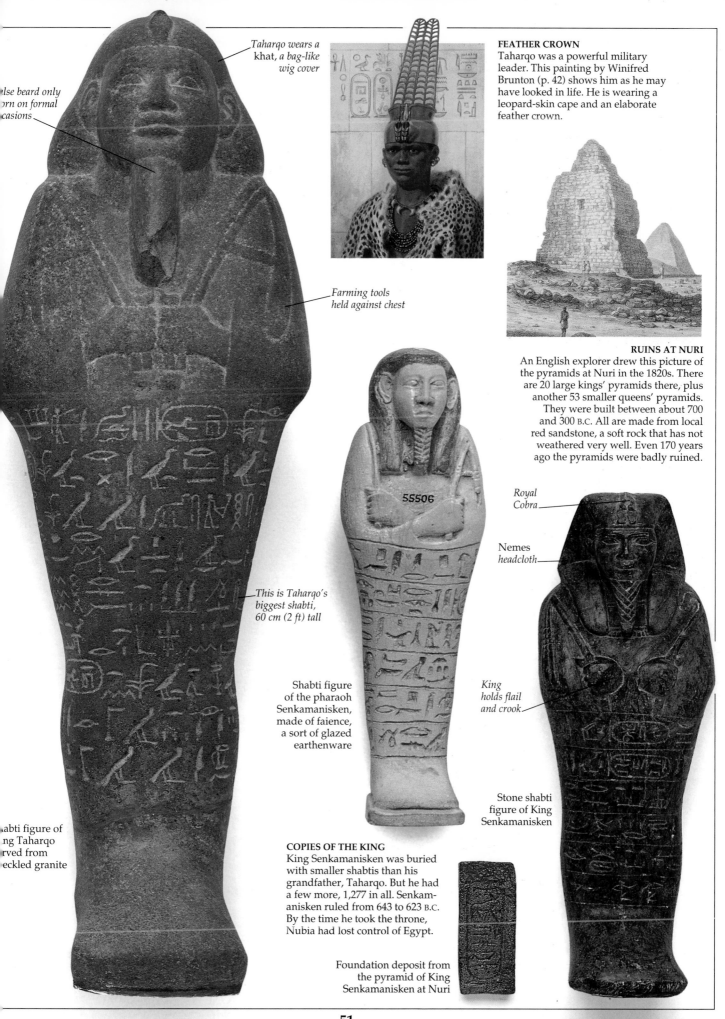

Taharqo wears a
khat, *a bag-like
wig cover*

..lse beard only
..rn on formal
..casions

FEATHER CROWN
Taharqo was a powerful military
leader. This painting by Winifred
Brunton (p. 42) shows him as he may
have looked in life. He is wearing a
leopard-skin cape and an elaborate
feather crown.

*Farming tools
held against chest*

RUINS AT NURI
An English explorer drew this picture of
the pyramids at Nuri in the 1820s. There
are 20 large kings' pyramids there, plus
another 53 smaller queens' pyramids.
They were built between about 700
and 300 B.C. All are made from local
red sandstone, a soft rock that has not
weathered very well. Even 170 years
ago the pyramids were badly ruined.

55506

*Royal
Cobra*

*Nemes
headcloth*

This is Taharqo's
biggest shabti,
60 cm (2 ft) tall

Shabti figure
of the pharaoh
Senkamanisken,
made of faience,
a sort of glazed
earthenware

*King
holds flail
and crook*

Stone shabti
figure of King
Senkamanisken

..abti figure of
..ng Taharqo
..rved from
..eckled granite

COPIES OF THE KING
King Senkamanisken was buried
with smaller shabtis than his
grandfather, Taharqo. But he had
a few more, 1,277 in all. Senkamanisken ruled from 643 to 623 B.C.
By the time he took the throne,
Nubia had lost control of Egypt.

Foundation deposit from
the pyramid of King
Senkamanisken at Nuri

A queen's treasure

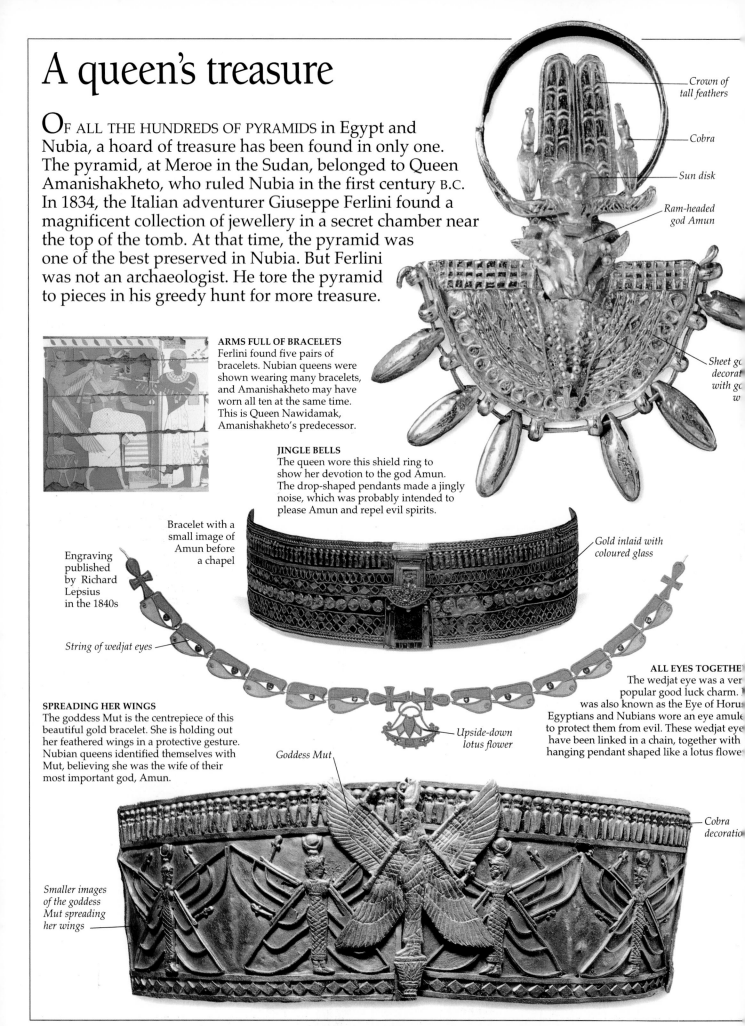

OF ALL THE HUNDREDS OF PYRAMIDS in Egypt and Nubia, a hoard of treasure has been found in only one. The pyramid, at Meroe in the Sudan, belonged to Queen Amanishakheto, who ruled Nubia in the first century B.C. In 1834, the Italian adventurer Giuseppe Ferlini found a magnificent collection of jewellery in a secret chamber near the top of the tomb. At that time, the pyramid was one of the best preserved in Nubia. But Ferlini was not an archaeologist. He tore the pyramid to pieces in his greedy hunt for more treasure.

Crown of tall feathers

Cobra

Sun disk

Ram-headed god Amun

Sheet go decorat with go w

ARMS FULL OF BRACELETS
Ferlini found five pairs of bracelets. Nubian queens were shown wearing many bracelets, and Amanishakheto may have worn all ten at the same time. This is Queen Nawidamak, Amanishakheto's predecessor.

JINGLE BELLS
The queen wore this shield ring to show her devotion to the god Amun. The drop-shaped pendants made a jingly noise, which was probably intended to please Amun and repel evil spirits.

Bracelet with a small image of Amun before a chapel

Engraving published by Richard Lepsius in the 1840s

Gold inlaid with coloured glass

String of wedjat eyes

ALL EYES TOGETHE
The wedjat eye was a ver popular good luck charm. was also known as the Eye of Horu Egyptians and Nubians wore an eye amule to protect them from evil. These wedjat eye have been linked in a chain, together with hanging pendant shaped like a lotus flowe

SPREADING HER WINGS
The goddess Mut is the centrepiece of this beautiful gold bracelet. She is holding out her feathered wings in a protective gesture. Nubian queens identified themselves with Mut, believing she was the wife of their most important god, Amun.

Upside-down lotus flower

Goddess Mut

Smaller images of the goddess Mut spreading her wings

Cobra decoratio

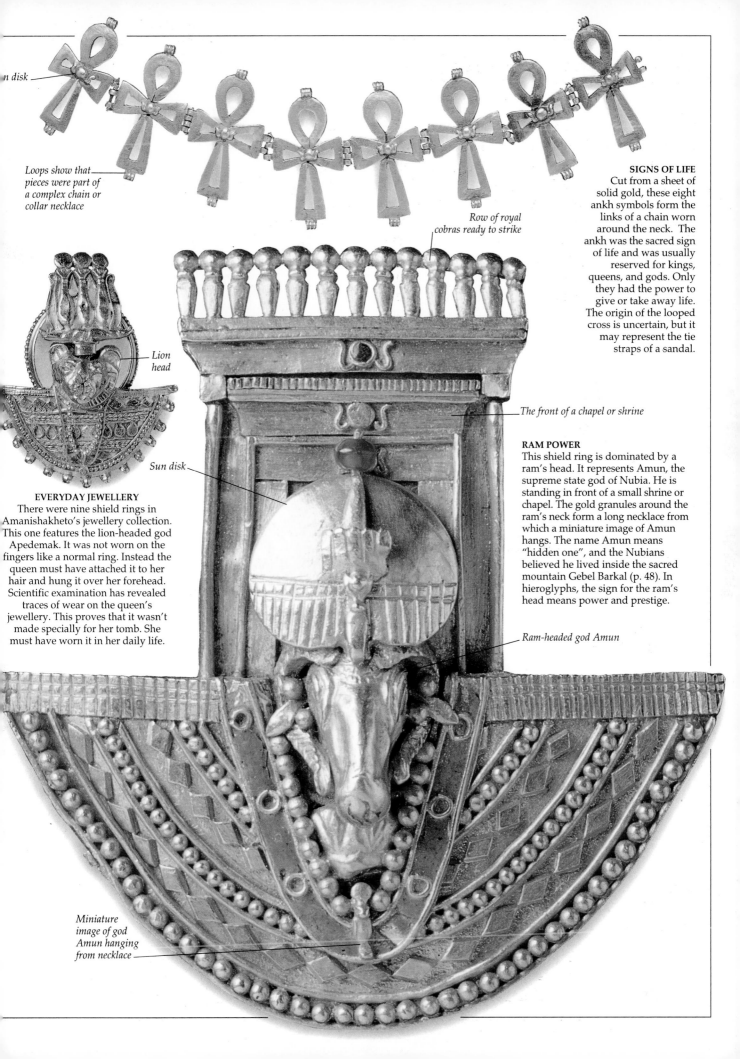

n disk

Loops show that
pieces were part of
a complex chain or
collar necklace

Row of royal
cobras ready to strike

SIGNS OF LIFE
Cut from a sheet of
solid gold, these eight
ankh symbols form the
links of a chain worn
around the neck. The
ankh was the sacred sign
of life and was usually
reserved for kings,
queens, and gods. Only
they had the power to
give or take away life.
The origin of the looped
cross is uncertain, but it
may represent the tie
straps of a sandal.

Lion
head

The front of a chapel or shrine

Sun disk

EVERYDAY JEWELLERY
There were nine shield rings in
Amanishakheto's jewellery collection.
This one features the lion-headed god
Apedemak. It was not worn on the
fingers like a normal ring. Instead the
queen must have attached it to her
hair and hung it over her forehead.
Scientific examination has revealed
traces of wear on the queen's
jewellery. This proves that it wasn't
made specially for her tomb. She
must have worn it in her daily life.

RAM POWER
This shield ring is dominated by a
ram's head. It represents Amun, the
supreme state god of Nubia. He is
standing in front of a small shrine or
chapel. The gold granules around the
ram's neck form a long necklace from
which a miniature image of Amun
hangs. The name Amun means
"hidden one", and the Nubians
believed he lived inside the sacred
mountain Gebel Barkal (p. 48). In
hieroglyphs, the sign for the ram's
head means power and prestige.

Ram-headed god Amun

Miniature
image of god
Amun hanging
from necklace

Pyramids of Mexico

Before the arrival of Europeans, Mexico and Central America were home to a wide variety of different peoples and empires. Over the centuries they built thousands of pyramids, usually with steps or terraces rising to a flat top. Most of the pyramids were temples, often arranged in complexes with many smaller religious buildings. Priests climbed the stairs to high altars where they conducted sacred rites, including human sacrifice. A few pyramids were constructed over tombs. Some of the most magnificent structures were built by the Mayan people in southern Mexico between the 3rd and 9th centuries A.D. The great Aztec pyramids were destroyed by the Spanish *conquistadors* (conquerors) who invaded Mexico in 1519.

OLMEC FROW
The Olmecs created the first great civilization of ancient Mexico. They were highly skilled at stone-working, and built massive earthen pyramid mounds at La Venta as early as 1000 B.C. They also carved beautiful masks as offerings to their gods. These have hug features and are usually frowning. The Olmecs' religious beliefs influenced lat culture like the Mayas and Zapotecs.

THE BIG ONES
Here are some major pyramid sites in Central America. It is not a huge area, but it includes high, cool valleys and steamy lowland jungles. Many sites have never been excavated. For instance, hundreds of small pyramids are still hidden in the dense jungle of Belize and the Yucatán Peninsula.

MEANWHILE, IN SOUTH AMERICA...
On the north coast of Peru, the Moche people built two great pyramids, the Huaca del Sol and the Huaca del Luna. They used sun-baked mud bricks laid in courses. The pyramids had two or three levels, and were coated in plaster and painted with colourful murals. The Moche also made fine pots. This one is shaped like a warrior.

COMPARING SIZES
The bases of the Pyramid of the Sun at Teotihuacan and the Great Pyramid of Egypt are almost the same size. But the Mexican pyramid is only about half as high. It is made of about 2.5 million tonnes of stone and earth, compared to 6.5 million tonnes of stone in the Great Pyramid.

CITY OF THE GODS
Teotihuacan is the most impressive ancient city in the Americas. This huge metropolis may once have been home to 250,000 people. Its many buildings and pyramids are carefully laid out on a strict grid plan. The wide Avenue of the Dead runs between the two biggest structures, the Pyramid of the Sun and the Pyramid of the Moon. This is the Pyramid of the Sun, built around A.D. 150. It appears to have no internal chambers, though there is a cave inside it. So who built this great city? When the Spanish asked the Aztecs, they said "the gods".

RAIN TOWN

Between A.D. 300 and 900, the city of El Tajín was the most important centre on the Veracruz coast of Mexico. This lush area was famous for its maize, cocoa, and cotton. The town itself was named after the rain god, Tajín. This imaginative painting by the Mexican artist Diego Rivera (1886–1957) shows two pyramids. The one on the right is the Pyramid of the Niches.

A detail from the fresco *Offering of Fruits, Tobacco, Cacao and Vanilla to the Emperor,* by Diego Rivera, 1950.

A NICHE A DAY

The Pyramid of the Niches at El Tajín rises in six tiers. Each tier contains rows of niches. There are 365 in all, one for each day of the year. Offerings or figures of gods may have been placed in the niches.

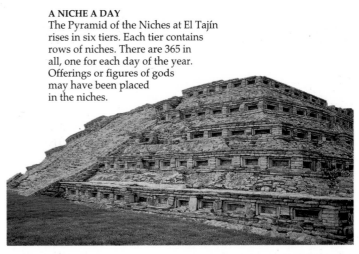

ZAPOTEC GOD

The Zapotec people made their capital at Monte Albán in the Oaxaca region of Mexico. Between 600 B.C. and A.D. 800, they built a remarkable city of pyramid temples and tombs there. The tombs have niches where clay funerary urns were placed. On this urn the rain god Cocijo wears a typical Zapotec feathered headdress.

Elaborate feathered headdress

Urn was built up from layers of clay slabs

The rain god Cocijo, wearing ear studs and sticking out his forked tongue

Urn is made around a cylinder that held food offerings or ashes

Mayan pyramids

BETWEEN THE 3RD AND 9TH CENTURIES A.D., the Mayas built pyramids all across eastern Mexico and into modern Belize, Guatemala, Honduras, and El Salvador. Made of stone block held together with strong lime mortar, Mayan pyramids were built at steeper angles than Egyptian ones. The staircases sometimes got narrower as they rose, to make the pyramids seem even taller and steeper. This also drew attention to the rituals performed in the temple chamber at the top. Crowds gathered at the base, but only priests could climb to the sacred heights. The Mayas were skilled astronomers and laid out their pyramids according to the sun, moon, and stars. They also developed yearly and sacred calendars, a system of mathematics, and their own language of picture-writing or "glyphs". This has still not been fully deciphered.

CITY KINGDOM
The Maya did not have a single capital or king. Instead each city governed itself under its own ruler. One important later city was Chichén Itzá in the Yucatán Peninsula. There were many major religious and administrative buildings there, including the famous pyramid El Castillo. The stone pillars in the architecture show the influence of the Toltecs, a neighbouring culture. People were thrown to their deaths in the sacred Well of Sacrifice.

DANCING GODS
These drawings show two gods shared by most Central American people. On his nightly journey beneath the earth, the Sun god became the jaguar god of the underworld. The black spots on his fur symbolized the stars. The serpent Quetzalcoatl was thought to express sacred power. A person's head is often shown emerging from his open mouth, to link this sacred creature to the human world.

Jaguar god

Quetzalcoatl

JAGUAR POT
Very few Mayan wall paintings remain. But we can get some idea of their quality from the decorated ceramics that have survived. Pots for the rich or for religious use were covered with stucco and then painted while still wet. This one shows a jaguar, admired for its skill in hunting and its strength, ferocity, and cunning.

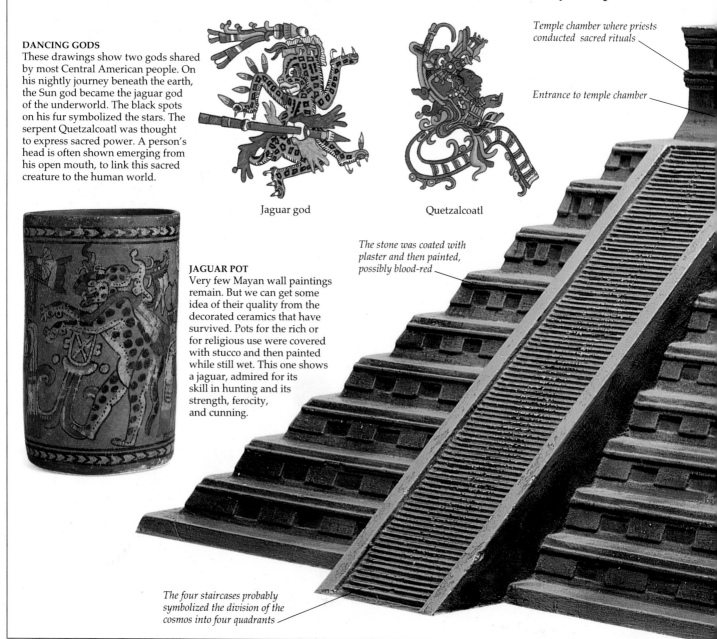

Temple chamber where priests conducted sacred rituals

Entrance to temple chamber

The stone was coated with plaster and then painted, possibly blood-red

The four staircases probably symbolized the division of the cosmos into four quadrants

FEATHERED SERPENT
The first known god of Mexico was Quetzalcoatl, the feathered serpent. This is one of the seven serpent figures on the northern stairs of El Castillo pyramid at Chichén Itzá. At the autumn equinox, around 23 September every year, the sun shines through the mouths of all seven serpents.

...ACKING THE CODE
...over a hundred years, researchers struggled to understand ...mysterious Mayan glyphs. Only in the last twenty years ...e they started to break the code. There are many stone ...criptions. But most of the Mayan books, called codices, ...re burned in 1562 by a Spanish priest who claimed they ...re the works of the devil. Only four survived. These were ...itten and painted on bark paper folded in sections. They ...e helped us to understand the Mayan calendars and ...thematics. These five gods are from the Codex Tro-...rtesianus. The bars and dots are glyphs for numbers.

LOST CITIES
In the 800s, the Mayan civilization went through a spectacular collapse. No one really knows why. Ravaged by war and famine, the cities were abandoned one by one. The jungle plants took over the temples and the statues were swallowed by the undergrowth. These lost cities were only rediscovered recently. This is a photo of El Castillo pyramid at Chichén Itzá, taken by an English explorer around 1900.

Pyramid is 24 m (79 ft) high

STEPPING THE DAYS AWAY
This model shows El Castillo pyramid at Chichén Itzá. It has four staircases, three with 91 steps and one with 92. That makes a total of 365 steps, one for each day of the year.

Single northern staircase on inner Toltec pyramid

Outer Mayan pyramid has four staircases

INNER TEMPLES
Mexican pyramids were often enlarged by new rulers. In this way, they grew bigger and bigger. In 1930, Mexican archaeologists discovered an earlier temple inside Chichén Itzá pyramid. Probably built by the Toltecs, it also has nine levels, but only one staircase. Inside the temple chamber are a magnificent jaguar throne and a sculpture on which offerings were placed.

Nine terraces

Continued on next page

Blood-letting and sacrifice

Bloody rituals were a vital part of Mayan life. They believed that to keep the cosmic order, the gods needed to be fed with blood. In return, the gods would provide good harvests and prevent natural disasters like earthquakes. One mural shows prisoners of war being tortured by having their fingernails pulled out. Human sacrifice may have been introduced to the Mayas by the war-like Toltecs. The victims were prisoners of war, slaves, or children bought especially for the occasion. The priest who performed the sacrifice was helped by four old men who held the victim's arms and legs while the chest was ripped open. The priests performed these sacrifices during special festivals in the sacred calendar.

SPILLING YOUR OWN BLOOD
Mayan nobles mutilated themselves in special blood-letting ceremonies. They passed needles or stingray spines through parts of the body and collected the blood to smear on statues. Men usually pierced their penises. This sculpture from Yaxchilán (south of Tikal) shows Lady Xoc passing a string of thorns through her tongue. The ruler Shield Jaguar looks on.

Glyphs from a wood beam on the Temple the Giant Jaguar, Tik Guatemala

PUBLIC ADDRESS
There are five major pyramid complexes at Tikal, Guatemala. This is the Temple of the Giant Jaguar, the tallest of all the Mayan pyramids. It rises steeply to a height of 70 m (230 ft). The chamber at the top was designed to amplify the priests' voices, so they could be heard by spectators at the base. The tomb of a Mayan lord, Ah Cacan, was beneath the pyramid.

OVAL PYRAMID
The Pyramid of the Magician at Uxmal, Mexico, has curved walls. It was built in five distinct phases from the 6th to 10th centuries. The ceremonial stairway on the west side leads to the broad temple chamber. The entrance is richly decorated, and looks like the mouth of a great monster.

DOORWAY TO DATES
Mayan temple doors were spanned by wooden beams. The wood can be dated by the radiocarbon process. This helps experts to confirm the dates of Mayan history, which are still not very clear. These details from a wooden beam are glyphs.

Glyph from a wooden beam on the Temple of the Giant Jaguar, Tikal, Guatemala

King, wearing a feathered crown

Members of the royal family

Nobles, priests, and warriors

Merchants, artists, and craftsworkers

Peasant farmers, labourers, and slaves

MAYAN SOCIAL PYRAMID
A modern Mexican artist painted this pyramid to show the different classes of Mayan society. It is done in the style of the beautiful frescoes found at Bonampak, Guatemala. Each important Mayan city had its own ruler or king, who was regarded by his people as a living god. To live up to his reputation, the king built splendid palaces and temples.

JUNGLE RUINS
Between 1839 and 1842, John Stephens and Frederick Catherwood made two famous expeditions to explore Mayan ruins. Jungle travel was dangerous, and they both suffered bad bouts of malaria. Their writings and drawings revealed the full splendour of the lost civilization. This lithograph shows a pyramid in Tulum, Mexico.

MYSTERIOUS GODS
This is a reconstruction of a frieze from Campeche, Mexico. Traces of colour suggest that the original was brightly painted. Very little is known about the bewildering variety of Mayan gods.

Aztec pyramids

THE AZTECS RULED the last great empire of Central America. They called themselves *Mexica* and made their capital at Tenochtitlán, now Mexico City. When the Spanish *conquistadors* entered Tenochtitlán in 1519, they found one of the largest cities in the world. They were impressed by its beauty, cleanliness, and order. But as they approached the huge ceremonial centre, the Spaniards were horrified by the smell of blood. The Aztecs used their pyramids for human sacrifice, which they believed provided vital energy needed for the workings of the universe. In the last years of their empire, thousands of victims, mostly prisoners of war, were sacrificed each year. The Aztecs built their pyramids from a core of adobe mud bricks faced with stone held together by mortar. None of them were very high. The tallest, the Great Temple of Tenochtitlán, was only a fifth of the height of the Great Pyramid at Giza.

Tezcatlipoca

Huitzilopochtli

REPAYING THE GODS
The top of the pyramid was a place of bloody sacrifice. Here the priests removed the still-beating heart of the victim. Then they threw the body down the steps, and the limbs were hacked off and ceremonially eaten. The Aztecs believed that the world had been created by their gods' own sacrifice. These terrible rituals were their gifts of thanks.

The snake was associated with the god Quetzalcoatl, whose name meant "feathered serpent"

SACRIFICIAL KNIFE
The victim's heart was cut out with a stone knife. The Aztecs had no iron and made their tools from razor-sharp flint or obsidian, a volcanic glass. This flint blade is decorated with a turquoise mosaic of a snake, a symbol of sacred power. The Aztecs excelled at mosaic work using jade, coral, shell, and turquoise.

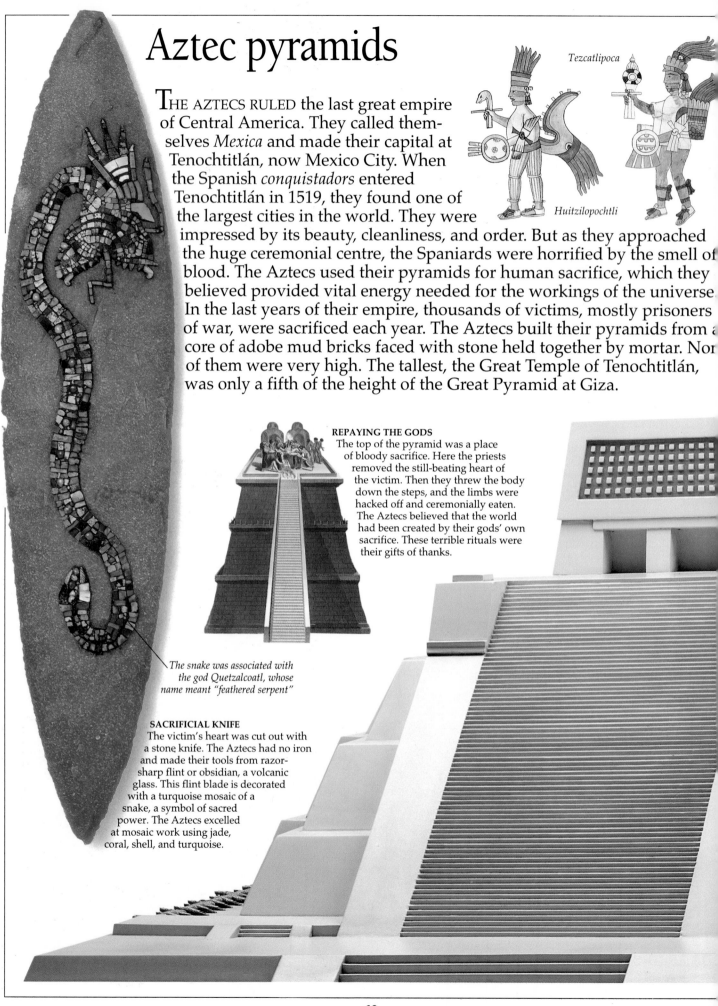

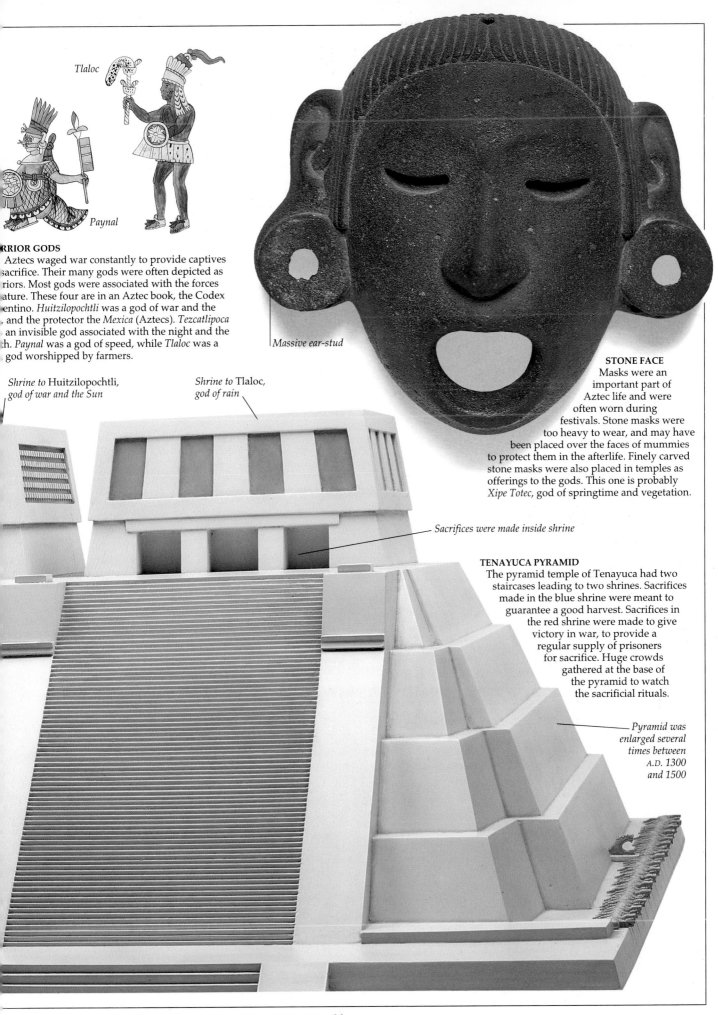

Tlaloc

Paynal

RRIOR GODS

Aztecs waged war constantly to provide captives
sacrifice. Their many gods were often depicted as
riors. Most gods were associated with the forces
ature. These four are in an Aztec book, the Codex
entino. *Huitzilopochtli* was a god of war and the
, and the protector the *Mexica* (Aztecs). *Tezcatlipoca*
an invisible god associated with the night and the
h. *Paynal* was a god of speed, while *Tlaloc* was a
god worshipped by farmers.

Massive ear-stud

STONE FACE

Masks were an
important part of
Aztec life and were
often worn during
festivals. Stone masks were
too heavy to wear, and may have
been placed over the faces of mummies
to protect them in the afterlife. Finely carved
stone masks were also placed in temples as
offerings to the gods. This one is probably
Xipe Totec, god of springtime and vegetation.

Shrine to Huitzilopochtli,
god of war and the Sun

Shrine to Tlaloc,
god of rain

Sacrifices were made inside shrine

TENAYUCA PYRAMID

The pyramid temple of Tenayuca had two
staircases leading to two shrines. Sacrifices
made in the blue shrine were meant to
guarantee a good harvest. Sacrifices in
the red shrine were made to give
victory in war, to provide a
regular supply of prisoners
for sacrifice. Huge crowds
gathered at the base of
the pyramid to watch
the sacrificial rituals.

*Pyramid was
enlarged several
times between
A.D. 1300
and 1500*

61

The pyramid lives on…

FOUR AND A HALF THOUSAND YEARS after the Great Pyramid rose on Egypt's desert horizon, a different kind of pyramid is appearing on city skylines. Modern pyramids are not made of millions of tonnes of stone. It does not take thousands of workers to build them, and they represent big business, not the spiritual realm of the dead. New materials like reinforced concrete and smoked glass supported by steel girders mean that huge structures can be built with a minimum of effort. There is something special about the pyramid shape that has inspired architects, artists, and designers throughout history. As a geometric shape, it is the supreme symbol of natural balance and harmony. Built on a grand scale, it gives the impression of something superhuman, built by the gods. The eternal magic of the pyramid is destined to live on and on.

THE ROME PYRAM
The most impressive anci
pyramid in Europe is in Rome
was built by Caius Cestius,
important official who died in 12
He is buried beneath the pyram

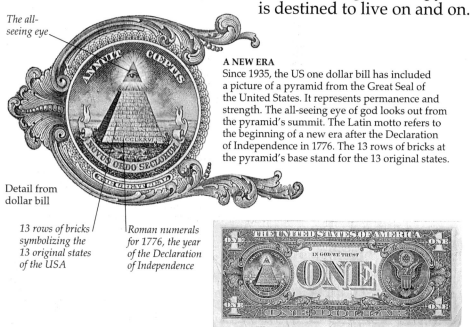

The all-seeing eye

A NEW ERA
Since 1935, the US one dollar bill has included a picture of a pyramid from the Great Seal of the United States. It represents permanence and strength. The all-seeing eye of god looks out from the pyramid's summit. The Latin motto refers to the beginning of a new era after the Declaration of Independence in 1776. The 13 rows of bricks at the pyramid's base stand for the 13 original states.

Detail from
dollar bill

13 rows of bricks symbolizing the 13 original states of the USA

Roman numerals for 1776, the year of the Declaration of Independence

PYRAMID POWER
This greenhouse is in the botanical garde
in Sydney, Australia. The pyramid shape
ensures that a large surface area of glass
faces the sun. But many people believe
that the shape itself can generate hidden
power or energy. They claim that a blunt
razor blade left at the centre of a pyramid
will be miraculously sharpened!

One dollar bill from United States of America

SETTING THE SCENE
The simple elegance of ancient Egyptian art has inspired many modern artists. The British artist David Hockney designed stage sets for Mozart's opera the Magic Flute in 1978. He used the pyramid shape to create a modern sense of grandeur.

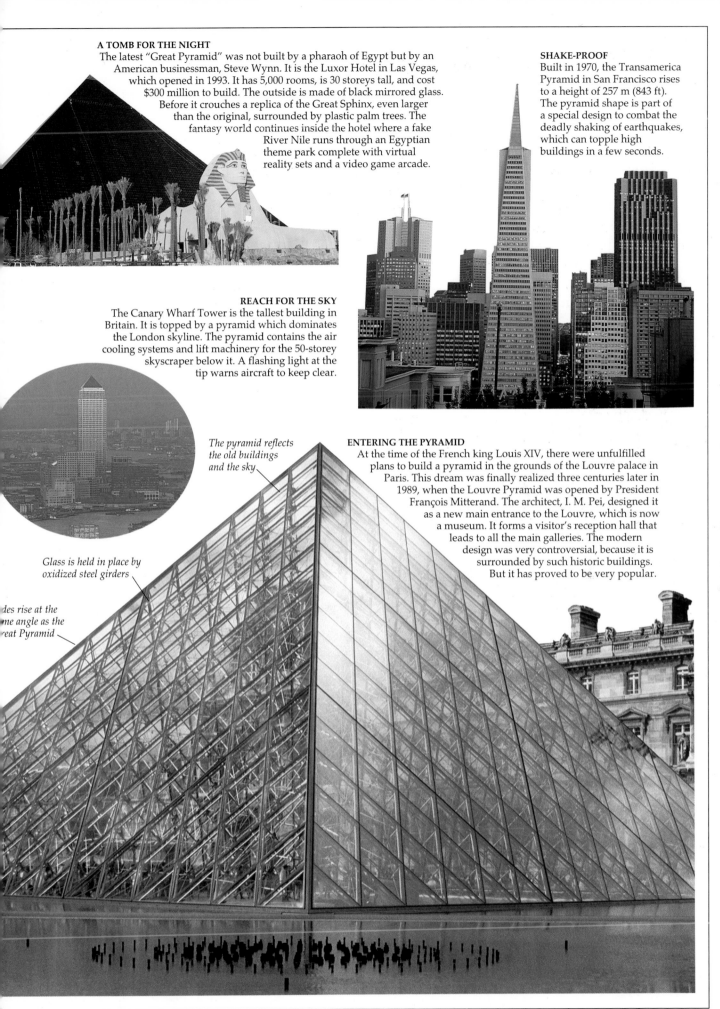

A TOMB FOR THE NIGHT

The latest "Great Pyramid" was not built by a pharaoh of Egypt but by an American businessman, Steve Wynn. It is the Luxor Hotel in Las Vegas, which opened in 1993. It has 5,000 rooms, is 30 storeys tall, and cost $300 million to build. The outside is made of black mirrored glass. Before it crouches a replica of the Great Sphinx, even larger than the original, surrounded by plastic palm trees. The fantasy world continues inside the hotel where a fake River Nile runs through an Egyptian theme park complete with virtual reality sets and a video game arcade.

SHAKE-PROOF

Built in 1970, the Transamerica Pyramid in San Francisco rises to a height of 257 m (843 ft). The pyramid shape is part of a special design to combat the deadly shaking of earthquakes, which can topple high buildings in a few seconds.

REACH FOR THE SKY

The Canary Wharf Tower is the tallest building in Britain. It is topped by a pyramid which dominates the London skyline. The pyramid contains the air cooling systems and lift machinery for the 50-storey skyscraper below it. A flashing light at the tip warns aircraft to keep clear.

The pyramid reflects the old buildings and the sky

ENTERING THE PYRAMID

At the time of the French king Louis XIV, there were unfulfilled plans to build a pyramid in the grounds of the Louvre palace in Paris. This dream was finally realized three centuries later in 1989, when the Louvre Pyramid was opened by President François Mitterand. The architect, I. M. Pei, designed it as a new main entrance to the Louvre, which is now a museum. It forms a visitor's reception hall that leads to all the main galleries. The modern design was very controversial, because it is surrounded by such historic buildings. But it has proved to be very popular.

Glass is held in place by oxidized steel girders

...des rise at the ...me angle as the ...eat Pyramid

Did you know?

FASCINATING FACTS

Pyramid of Khufu

Great Pyramid complex at Giza

▲ By the time of King Tutankhamun, Khufu's Great Pyramid at Giza (just outside modern-day Cairo) was more than 12 centuries old, and widely visited as a tourist attraction.

▲ Of the Seven Wonders of the Ancient World, the three pyramids at Giza were the oldest, yet they are the only one of these Wonders still in existence.

▲ According to ancient Egyptian hieroglyphic records, fresh garlic was fed to the labourers who were working on the pyramids to keep them strong and healthy.

▲ The pyramids were constructed with incredible accuracy. The foundations of the Great Pyramid, for example, are almost perfectly flat – the highest corner is only 1.3 cm (0.5 in) above the lowest corner. Similarly, the greatest difference in length between the four sides is only 4 cm (2 in).

▲ The Great Pyramid has a number of narrow shafts that lead to the outside. Some experts think these were aligned with major stars so the king's spirit could ascend directly to heaven. Others believe they are simply there for ventilation.

▲ Centuries of pyramid building and a number of poor harvests had a serious effect on the Egyptian economy, so pyramids built when the Old Kingdom was drawing to a close are much smaller than those of Khufu and Khafra.

▲ King Amenemhat III (1855-1808 B.C.) built two pyramids. The first one, at Dahshur, contains the tombs of at least three queens, but the pharaoh himself is not buried there; his remains are in his second pyramid at Hawara.

King Amenemhat III

▲ Mayan pyramids were often painted bright red, a colour that represented their belief that the gods sacrificed their own blood to give man life.

El Castillo

▲ When the Spanish explorers asked the Aztecs who built the city of Teotihuacan with its two huge pyramids, the natives replied, "the Gods".

Ancient Aztec pyramid temple

▲ The architects and engineers of ancient Egypt took only 400 years to progress from constructing primitive mastaba tombs to building huge, straight-sided pyramids. The last stage of this process – the leap from stepped to "true" pyramids – took only 65 years and constitutes one of the most astonishingly rapid technological advances in history.

▲ One structural factor likely to have influenced the distinctive form of the pyramids is the fact that, before the Romans invented concrete, no other shape could be constructed on such a vast scale, yet still remain strong and stable.

▲ In the early nineteenth century, a sarcophagus was discovered inside Menkaura's pyramid, but it was lost at sea on its way to the British Museum.

El Castillo, the Mayan pyramid at Chichén Itzá in Mexico, was once covered in plaster and red paint.

QUESTIONS AND ANSWERS

Q When did we first learn about Egyptian pyramids?

A Worldwide fascination with the tombs of the ancient pharaohs was sparked off when Napoleon's troops discovered them during his north African campaign. In 1798, he commissioned a study of Egyptian culture that involved 150 artists, scientists and engineers, and provided the foundation of all our modern knowledge.

Q What spiritual factors inspired the shape of the pyramids?

A Most straight-sided pyramids are associated with sun worship, and their sloping sides were intended to echo beams of light. In Egypt, the rising planes also formed a pathway to heaven for the pharaoh's spirit to follow.

Q Have the pyramids at Giza always looked the way they do now?

A No; when the three pyramids were first built, they were surrounded by smaller buildings such as temples, mastaba tombs for important nobles of the court, and small queens' pyramids in which the pharaohs' wives and and other members of the royal family were buried. Also, each pyramid would have been cased in smooth, white limestone that glittered in the sun.

Q Why are climbers banned from the outer walls of the Giza pyramids?

A Until fairly recently, tourists regularly climbed the Great Pyramid. This caused considerable damage to the structure, though, and to the individual stones, on which people carved or wrote their names. In addition, climbers were often injured on the steep sides and a few even committed suicide by jumping from the top. Since the 1980s, all climbing at the site has been forbidden.

Napoleon in Egypt by Antoine-Jean Gros

Q Why did the Aztecs offer human sacrifices on their pyramids?

A The Aztecs worshipped sun gods, and believed that without the constant nourishment of human blood, the sun would stop shining. Their pyramids were holy places with steep sides reaching up toward the sacred light. On the very top, the nearest place to the sun, priests would perform bloody sacrificial rites that involved ripping out their victims' hearts while still beating and – on one particular festival – stripping off their skin and wearing it like clothing.

Record Breakers

STACKED TOMBS
The first pyramid was built for the Egyptian pharaoh Djoser about 2650 B.C. Its distinctive stepped shape was a result of its simple construction: a number of mastabas (rectangular, flat-topped tombs) of decreasing size stacked on top of one another.

SUPER STRUCTURE
The Great Pyramid at Giza is not only the largest pyramid in the world, but, 44 centuries after it was built, it is still the largest burial monument and the largest stone structure ever made.

STANDING TALL
Until the Eiffel Tower was completed in 1887, the Great Pyramid was also the tallest structure in existence.

LIFE'S WORK
Khufu's father, Sneferu, built at least three, maybe even four, pyramids. Although none of them was as big as his son's monument, together they represented an even more extensive construction project.

SOLID STONE
When it was finished, the Great Pyramid contained more stone than all the cathedrals of modern Europe existing today. There were 2,300,000 blocks in all, weighing an average of 2.5 tonnes (2.8 tons) each. The largest stones weighed about 15 tonnes (16.5 tons).

SACRED LIST
Among the earliest existing writings on papyrus are fragments of a list kept by scribes of all the offerings made at the pyramid temple of King Neferirkara (2475-2455 B.C.).

EARLY EXPLORATIONS
The first excavations at the Giza pyramids were made by King Tuthmosis IV in about 1400 B.C.

TALL, TALLER, TALLEST
Although it was the tallest of all the Aztec pyramids, the Great Temple at Tenochtitlan was only one fifth as tall as Khufu's Great Pyramid.

WRITING ON THE WALLS
The oldest known religious writings are sacred hieroglyphs called the Pyramid Texts. Dating from about 2340 B.C., these were found on the walls of some of the chambers inside King Unas' pyramid.

Eiffel Tower

The Pyramid Texts in the tomb of King Unas

King Djoser

Who's who?

THE PYRAMIDS OF THE ANCIENT WORLD were built on a scale so massive and overwhelming that it is easy to forget that the extraordinary power, skill and sheer strength behind them came from ordinary people. We know very little about the labourers who actually built these awesome monuments, nor, in most cases, can we identify the architects and engineers who designed them. What we do have, however, is a fascinating record of many of the ancient rulers who commissioned them.

PYRAMID BUILDERS

Pyramid Text on the walls of Unas' tomb

DJOSER

Third-dynasty king who built the first pyramid in about 2650 B.C. Stepped in structure, Djoser's historic tomb at Saqqara was the model for all the Egyptian pyramids that followed. His architect, the high priest Imhotep, pioneered the use of stone rather than mud brick for building.

SNEFURU

Fourth-dynasty pharaoh who built several pyramids for himself and his family, including the first example with smooth, as opposed to stepped, sides. Snefuru was the father of Khufu.

KHUFU

Sometimes known by his Greek name, Cheops, Khufu commissioned the largest tomb of all, the Great Pyramid, on the west bank of the Nile at Giza, about 2589 B.C.

Hieroglyphs from King Sahura's pyramid

KHAFRA

Thought to be Khufu's son – or possibly younger brother – Khafra built the second Giza pyramid. Although smaller than Khufu's, it looks taller since it is built on higher ground and its summit is still intact.

MENKAURA

Builder of the third, and smallest, Giza pyramid, Menkaura is believed to be Khafra's son. South of his pyramid, he placed three smaller "queens" pyramids for his wives and children.

SAHURA

Earliest fifth-dynasty king to be buried in a complex of pyramids at Abusir, south of Giza. Sahura's tomb is the best preserved at this site, and the only one open to visitors. Nearby is the pyramid of his brother and heir, Neferirkara, which is about the same size as Menkaura's at Giza.

UNAS

Final pharaoh of the fifth dynasty, Unas built his pyramid at the Saqqara complex. Today, his tomb is best known for the important hieroglyphic writings (called the Pyramid Texts) discovered on the walls of the burial chamber.

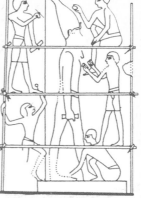

Rekhmire's tomb drawings

PEPY I AND II

Sixth-dynasty pharaohs whose comparatively small pyramids at Saqqara were the last to be built for over 200 years.

AMENEMHAT I

The first Middle-Kingdom king to construct a true pyramid. It was located at Lisht. Like all pyramids built during this era, Amenemhat I's was smaller and less well constructed than those of the Old Kingdom.

REKHMIRE

An official during the reigns of Tuthmosis III and Amenhotep II, Rekhmire was buried in a tomb that contained fascinating wall drawings illustrating details of pyramid construction.

TUTHMOSIS IV

Eighteenth-dynasty king who undertook early explorations of the Giza pyramids about 1400 B.C. Tuthmosis also made one of the first attempts to free the Sphinx from the drifting sands that had buried the figure up to its neck.

TAHARQO

Nubian king who ruled over both Nubia and Egypt during the 25th dynasty. Inspired by the Giza pyramids, Taharqo's huge monument at Nuri was one of 20 kings' pyramids and 53 queens' pyramids at the site.

AMANISHAKHETO

Nubian Queen during the first century B.C. whose pyramid, uniquely, was still full of treasures in the early nineteenth century.

PYRAMID EXPLORERS

THE KNOWLEDGE WE HAVE about the pyramids came to us largely through the efforts of intrepid explorers, archaeologists and historians of many nationalities who devoted their lives to uncovering the secrets of the pyramids.

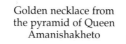

Golden necklace from the pyramid of Queen Amanishakheto

Herodotus

HERODOTUS

Greek historian who drew up one of the earliest accounts (about 450 B.C.) of how the pyramids were constructed. Later, some of his theories were disproved.

NAPOLEON BONAPARTE

After he invaded Egypt in 1798, Napoleon commissioned the first modern study of Egypt's ancient culture.

LUIGI MAYER

Italian adventurer whose illustrated volume *Views in Egypt* (published 1804) helped stimulate interest in Egypt's history.

JEAN-FRANCOIS CHAMPOLLION

French scholar, linguist and archaeologist responsible for the single largest contribution to Egyptology ever made, the deciphering of ancient hieroglyphics in 1822.

GIUSEPPE FERLINI

A notable villain in the history of Egyptology, Ferlini discovered a hoard of jewellery in Queen Amanishakheto's miraculously preserved pyramid in 1834. In his search for further riches, he damaged the structure irrevocably.

HOWARD VYSE

Author of one of the earliest and most famous reference books on the subject, *The Pyramids of Gizeh*, published in 1837.

W. M. FLINDERS PETRIE

English archaeologist who made the first detailed study of the Giza pyramids in 1881-82. Petrie also published over 1,000 books and papers and pioneered several techniques for pyramid exploration.

JEAN-PHILIPPE LAUER

Twentieth-century French architect and Egyptologist who devoted his life to reconstructing the Step Pyramid at Saqqara.

Jean-Philippe Lauer

FREDERICK CATHERWOOD AND JOHN LLOYD STEPHENS

Mid-nineteenth-century American explorers who discovered a number of ancient Mayan ruins in the Mexican jungle, and produced some of the first widely seen sketches of the distinctive pyramids of Central America. Stephens recorded their pioneering discoveries in two volumes of published diaries, which he called *Incidents of Travel*.

W. M. Flinders Petrie

AUGUSTE MARIETTE

Nineteenth-century French Egyptologist who discovered Khafa's Valley Temple at Giza and the Serapeum (burial chamber for sacred bulls) at Saqqara. Mariette went on to found the original Egyptian Museum at Cairo.

Nineteenth-century lithograph from Catherwood and Stephens' travels

Find out more

THE WEALTH OF TREASURES unearthed from ancient pyramids has made it possible for museums all over the world to put together collections of objects and artworks that communicate some of the magic of these ancient structures. There is also a wealth of printed material available. While you can readily find information on all the pyramids in Egypt and in Central America, the focus of much of the available material is the Giza plateau with its legendary Old Kingdom pyramids.

Dominated by the Great Pyramid and the Sphinx, the Giza complex once also contained temples, mastaba tombs, smaller pyramids and covered causeways. Today, it is surrounded by tourists, hawkers, beggars, and a daily Sound and Light show, yet the immense structures still make a powerful impression on those who visit them.

Limestone casing

The Sphinx has the body of a lion and the head of a man

Crumbled ruins of King Unas' pyramid

Pyramid of Khufu

ETERNAL WATCH
Guarded by its Sphinx, whose face was carved in the pharaoh's image, Khafra's pyramid is the only one that retains – at its tip – some of the limestone casing that originally covered all three tombs. The rest was removed by medieval rulers of Cairo, who used it for their own monuments. This is the view of the compl from the edge of the Giza Plateau.

RUINED MONUMENT
Just south of the enclosure walls at Saqqara is the ruined pyramid of King Unas, who ruled Egypt fro about 2375 to 2345 B.C. The entire Saqqara burial site which is south of Cairo near Memphis, originally extended for over 7 km (4 miles) from north to sout

IN HIS MASTER'S SHADOW
It was not only pharaohs and their families who were buried on the Giza plateau; important members of the royal household could also be laid to rest there. This tomb, with its starkly beautiful columns guarding the entrance, was built for Seshemnufer, one of Khufu's courtiers.

USEFUL WEBSITES

- General information site for ancient Egypt
  www.cairoo.com
- Outstanding site relating to Egyptian pyramids and including links to other websites
  www.egyptianpyramids.com
- Specialist Egyptian site run by the British Museum
  www.ancientEgypt.co.uk
- Official website of the Giza complex
  www.guardians.net/hawass/khufu.htm
- General site relating to Egyptian and Central American pyramids and designed for children
  www.school.discovery.com/homeworkhelp/worldbook/atozhistory/p/453060.html

Lotus-adorned
Egyptian vessel in
the British Museum

KULCAN'S CASTLE

Castillo (The Castle), at
ichén Itzá in Mexico, was
lt around 800 and dedicated
Kukulcan, the Mayan version
he ancient god Quetzalcoatl.
erall, the pyramid is 24 m
ft) high; the square
cture at the very top
ukulcan's temple.

TRICKS OF THE LIGHT

At the foot of El Castillo's north staircase are two serpents' heads, thought to represent the god Kukulcan himself. At both equinoxes, the play of light on the staircase makes it look as if these sacred creatures are crawling up the pyramid's steep façade.

OLS OF THE TRADE

ny of the implements used by
ient Egyptian pyramid builders
strikingly similar to their
dern equivalents. Then, as now,
rpenter's saw cut through
ber, while his chisel was used
detailed work such as carving
ages and hieroglyphs. The
mples below are both models
covered in the foundations of
uthmosis III's temple.

Chisel

Saw

Places to visit

GIZA PYRAMIDS, CAIRO, EGYPT

In the interests of preservation, and in order for necessary restoration to be done, the three pyramids are closed alternately to tourists. Some of the best sites to see are:
- the Great Gallery and the King's Chamber in the Great Pyramid of Khufu
- the Solar Boat Museum, which exhibits a full-sized boat discovered – in pieces – in a pit beside the Great Pyramid
- the remains of the mortuary temple, sanctuary and courtyard outside Khafra's tomb.

SAQQARA, NEAR MEMPHIS, EGYPT

Necropolis (burial ground) of the Old Kingdom capital of Memphis, Saqqara is one of the most important archaeological sites in Egypt. Among its treasures are:
- the step pyramid of King Djoser, prototype for all Egyptian pyramids
- the pyramid of the last fifth-dynasty king, Unas, which contains the important hieroglyphic inscriptions known as the Pyramid Texts.

ABUSIR, NEAR CAIRO, EGYPT

Less impressive in themselves than the Giza and Saqqara monuments, the fifth-dynasty pyramids at Abusir are set in a spectacular, and considerably less crowded, landscape. Of particular interest are:
- the pyramid of King Sahura, the best preserved in the complex and the only one open to visitors
- the exterior of the nearby pyramids of Nyuserra, Neferirkara and Raneferef and their ruined temples and causeways.

EGYPTIAN MUSEUM, CAIRO, EGYPT

As well as the treasures of Tutankhamun and the Royal Mummy Room, this museum has hundreds of artefacts relating to the pyramids, including:
- statues of the great pyramid builders Djoser and Khafra
- a collection of personal objects relating to Hetepheres, mother of Khufu, including a canopic jar that once contained her internal organs.

EL CASTILLO, CHICHEN ITZA, MEXICO

Built around 800, this Mayan temple dominates the Chichén Itzá site and affords a stunning view of the surrounding countryside. Visitors can see:
- the serpents' heads at the bottom of the north staircase, which are believed to represent the god Kukulcan, Mayan version of the Aztec Quetzalcoatl
- the temple at the top of the inner pyramid.

PYRAMIDS OF THE SUN AND MOON, TEOTIHUACAN, MEXICO

Completed during the second century, these stepped pyramids are made of adobe bricks and earth, faced with gravel and stone. Worth investigating are:
- the on-site museum, which displays a scale model of the ancient city
- the view from the top of the Pyramid of the Moon.

Glossary

ADZE Ancient Egyptian tool for carving and planing wood.

ANCIENT EGYPT The period when Egypt was ruled by pharaohs, which was between around 3100 B.C and 30 B.C.

ANKH Ancient Egyptian symbol of life, which, traditionally, only gods and royalty carried.

ANTECHAMBER Small room that leads to a bigger or more important one.

ARTEFACT Ancient man-made object usually unearthed during archaeological explorations.

AZTECS Central American civilization that dominated Mexico before the Spanish conquest in the sixteenth century.

BONING RODS Pair of cylinders joined by a length of string, and used to establish a smooth flat surface on the stone sides of a true pyramid.

Adze

Capital

CAPITAL The top section of an architectural column, which in ancient Egypt was often shaped like a locally growing plant or flower, such as palm or papyrus.

Ancient Egyptian frieze

CAPSTONE The finishing stone on top of a pyramid or wall.

CARTOUCHE In Egyptology, an oval border enclosing a Pharaoh's name.

CASING Covering layer of smooth, fine stone on the outside of a building.

CATARACT Powerful rush of water around a large rock that blocks a river's flow. There are several cataracts along the Nile, and important monuments were often sited near them.

CAUSEWAY Raised road across a low or wet area of ground or a body of water.

CENOTAPH Memorial monument to a single person or a group of people who are buried elsewhere.

CODICES Ancient manuscript texts in book form.

COLONNADE Row of architectural columns supporting arches or a decorative upper surface.

CONQUISTADOR A Spanish invader, or conqueror, who plundered Central and South America during the sixteenth century.

CUBIT Basic unit of measurement in ancient Egypt, equal to the length from the elbow to the tip of the thumb (52.4 cm or 20.62 in). Each cubit was divided into seven palms, each palm containing four digits.

DOLERITE Extremely hard, coarse rock used in the process of quarrying stone.

FRIEZE Broad horizontal band of decoration on a wall.

GLYPHS Pictorial images used instead of words by the Mayan civilization of Central America.

HIEROGLYPHS Picture writing used to build up words in ancient Egyptian script.

INCAS South American civilization that flourished in Peru before the Spanish conquest in the sixteenth century.

KHAT Bag-like cover worn over a pharaoh's wig.

Model of a conquistador on horseback and a foot soldier

LABYRINTH Intricate and confusing network of passages.

LAPIS LAZULI Bright blue semi-precious stone commonly found in Egyptian jewellery and artefacts.

LOTUS Waterlily whose shape was widely used as a decorative device in ancient Egypt.

MASTABA Early Egyptian tomb, made of sun-dried mud bricks and stone. Mastabas are oblong in shape with low, sloping sides and a flat roof.

MAYAS Advanced Central American culture that collapsed mysteriously during the 800s. The Mayan people were renowned pyramid builders.

MUMMY Dead body that has been preserved from decay, either naturally or by artificial means.

NICHE Shallow recess in a wall intended for display or storage. The Pyramid of the Niches in Mexico has 365 recesses, which may have held religious figures or offerings to the gods.

OBELISK Tapered stone column with a square or rectangular base and sloping sides rising to a pointed tip.

OBSIDIAN Glassy rock formed from solidified lava used for decoration and as a mirror. It also breaks to form an extremely sharp edge that was used to make cutting implements.

OSTRACON Fragment of stone or pottery inscribed with writing or drawing.

PALETTE Flat surface on which colours were mixed to make either writing pigments or cosmetics.

PAPYRUS Tall riverside reed whose stem was widely used to make baskets, sandals, boats, rope and paper-like sheets or scrolls for writing on.

The Living Pharaoh (Ramses II) by Winifred Brunton

PHARAOH The title given to the rulers of ancient Egypt. The word pharaoh means "great house", and originally referred to the palace rather than the king.

PLAZA Open square or marketplace in a town or city.

PYRAMID Massive stone structure with a square base and sloping sides, which can be either straight or stepped. In ancient societies, pyramids were usually built as tombs, temples or monuments.

PYRAMIDION Cone-like capstone for the pointed roof of a scaled-down, pyramid-shaped tomb. These small brick structures were popular long after full-sized pyramids had fallen out of favour.

QUARRY Site where stone is extracted from the ground to be used for buildings, monuments or sculptures.

QUEEN'S PYRAMID Small pyramid built near a major one to contain the remains of a pharaoh's wives and children, or to fulfil an unknown symbolic function.

SARCOPHAGUS Elaborate outer coffin.

SACRIFICE The killing of people or animals as part of a religious ceremony. The Aztecs performed rites of human sacrifice to the sun gods on top of their Great Pyramid.

SCRIBE Government official who, unlike most ordinary people, could read and write.

SCHIST Layered metamorphic rock made up of sheets of different minerals that split into thin irregular plates.

SED COURT Elongated rectangular space in the step pyramid complexes where, watched by assembled crowds, pharaohs would traditionally run a course to test their fitness.

SEKED The angle of an Egyptian pyramid's sloping sides.

SERDAB Small chamber in a tomb intended to contain a statue of the deceased that his or her spirit could inhabit after death.

SHABTI Figures made in the image of servants, and often buried with important people so they could perform any manual tasks that were required in the afterlife. The word shabti comes from an Egyptian term meaning "to answer".

SLEDGE Flat surface on runners designed to carry heavy loads. When the pyramids were under construction, the building materials and stone blocks were transported to the sites on sledges.

SLIPWAY Artificial slope constructed beside a pyramid building site on which men and equipment could be transported.

SOUL HOUSE Miniature model dwelling placed in the tomb of its dead owner for use in the afterlife.

SPHINX In ancient Egypt, the sphinx was a monumental creature with a lion's body and the head of the ruler. Sphinxes were a symbol of royal power. They were believed to guard the entrances to the underworld on both the east and the west horizons.

STELA Upright stone slab or pillar covered with carvings or inscriptions.

STUCCO Durable, slow-setting plaster used as an outer covering on buildings or pieces of pottery.

TERRACE Raised level space near a building or in a garden, designed for walking or standing.

Tomb of the noble Seshemnufer in the shadow of the Great Pyramid

TOBE Egyptian word for brick, and the root of the word *adobe*, meaning sun-dried brick; type of building constructed from this material.

TOLTECS War-like people who inhabited Mexico before and during the time of the Aztecs. The Toltecs were also pyramid builders and they are suspected of introducing their pyramid rituals of human sacrifice to the Mayans.

TOMB Grave, monument or building where the body of a dead person is laid to rest.

VIZIERS The highest officials who were appointed by the pharaoh to rule over Upper and Lower Egypt.

WEDJET (WADJET) EYE Protective symbol widely used in ancient Egypt, which represents the eye of the sky-god Horus.

Great Stela at Axum

Index

Acknowledgements

Dorling Kindersley would like to thank:

The staff of the Department of Egyptian Antiquities at the British Museum, London, in particular John Taylor, Stephen Quirke, Carol Andrews, Jeffrey Spencer, Virginia Hewitt, Tony Brandon, Bob Dominey, and John Hayman; the British Museum Photographic Department, especially Ivor Kerslake; Angela Thomas and Arthur Boulton at the Bolton Museum; Robert Bauval; Jean-Phillipe Lauer; Helena Spiteri, and Linda Martin for editorial help; Sharon Spencer, Susan St. Louis, Isaac Zamora, and Ivan Finnegan for design help.

Additional photography by Peter Anderson (25ar, 36–37, 41br, 47l), Stan Bean (12–13), Janet Peckham (46cr), Dave Rudkin (55b), Karl Shone. **Maps** by Simone End (6cr, 8r, 54c)

Illustrations by John Woodcock (18bl, 21t, 41c, 54br), Sergio Momo (54c)

Index by Hilary Bird

Picture credits t=top b=bottom m=middle l=left r=right
Ayeesah Abdel-Haleem: 22br. Ancient Art and Architecture Collection: 37ar, 41ar; Stan Bean / Egyptian Museum, San José, Ca: 12-13b; Biblioteca Medicea Laurenziania / Photo - Scardigli: 60ar, 61al; Phot. Bibl. Nat., Paris / Codex Telleriano-Remensis: 61cl. The Ancient Egypt Picture Library: Robert Partridge 65tc. Bibliothèque du Musée de l'Homme: 57ac. British Museum: 67crа. J.Allan Cash Photolibrary: 62cr. J.L.Charmet: 59cl. G. Dagli Orti: 59ar.

Vivien Davis: 48cl, 48-49b. e.t.archive: 7c, 22cl, (detail) 43bl, 55ar. Mary Evans Picture Library: 16al, 17cr, 20bl, 22al, 47c, 60c. Francis Firth/Royal Photographic Society, Bath (The Southern stone pyramid of Dahshoor from the South West): 14cr. Gallimard Jeunesse: 17ar, 18c. Robert Harding Picture Library: 47br, 63al, 63ar; Gavin Hellier 64cra; © David Hockney / Photo-Guy Gravett: 62bl. Hutchison Library: 6bl, 58cl, / Pate: 6ar, 57ar. Image Bank / Luis Castañeda: 58ac, / Derek Berwin: 63cl. INAH: 57al. H.Lewandowski / Photo - R.M.N.: 9al. Jürgen Liepe: 11br, 18al, 18cr, 38br, 39cl, 46cl. Mansell Collection: (detail) 21br, 37cr, 38cl. ©Metropolitan Museum of Art, Gift of Edward S. Harkness, 1914 (14.3.17): 40l. Daniel Moignot, P.L.J. Gallimard-Larousse: 37al; Museum Expedition. Courtesy of Museum of Fine Arts, Boston: 19r. National Palace, Mexico City / Photo - e.t. archive (detail, Diego Rivera 'Totonac Civilisation') - Reproduccion authorizada por el Instituto

Nacional de Bellas Artes y Literatura: 55al. James Putnam: 7cr, 17al, 19al, 20ar, 21c, 42cl, 43cl, 51ac. R.M.N: 25br. John Ross: 12al. Royal Museum of Scotland: 56bl. Royal Observatory, Edinburgh: 47 ar. John Sandford/Science Photo Library: 47acr. Staatliche Museen zu Berlin Preussischer Kulturbesitz Agyptisches Museum / Photo - Margarete Busing / Bildarchiv: 52ar, 52b, 52c, 53a, 53b, 53br. Tony Stone Images: 63b. Werner Forman Archive: 14ar, 15al, 22bl, 31cl, 32cr, (detail) 35cl, (detail) 35ac, 39ar. Michel Zabé: 56-57b, 57cr, 58-59b, 60-61b. Zefa: 54bl, / J.Schörken: 56al.

Jacket credits
Back: British Museum
Front: Stone / Getty Images: Will and Denny Macintyre
British Museum: tc

All other images © Dorling Kindersley. For further information see: www.dkimages.com